I0766072

1

Blessed is the man that walketh not in the counsel of the ungodly, nor standeth in the way of sinners, nor sitteth in the seat of the scornful. 1:2 But his delight is in the law of the **LORD**; and in his law doth he meditate day and night. 1:3 And he shall be like a tree planted by the rivers of water, that bringeth forth his fruit in his season; his leaf also shall not wither; and whatsoever he doeth shall prosper. 1:4 The ungodly are not so: but are like the chaff which the wind driveth away. 1:5 Therefore the ungodly shall not stand in the judgment, nor sinners in the congregation of the righteous. 1:6 For the **LORD** knoweth the way of the righteous: but the way of the ungodly shall perish.

2

Why do the heathen rage, and the people imagine a vain thing? 2:2 The kings of the earth set themselves, and the rulers take counsel together, against the **LORD**, and against his anointed, saying, 2:3 Let us break their bands asunder, and cast away their cords from us. 2:4 He that sitteth in the heavens shall laugh: the LORD shall have them in derision. 2:5 Then shall he speak unto them in his wrath, and vex them in his sore displeasure. 2:6 Yet have I set my king upon my holy hill of Zion. 2:7 I will declare the decree: the LORD hath said unto me, Thou art my Son; this day have I begotten thee. 2:8 Ask of me, and I shall give thee the heathen for thine inheritance, and the uttermost parts of the earth for thy possession. 2:9 Thou shalt break them with a rod of iron; thou shalt dash them in pieces like a potter's vessel. 2:10 Be wise now therefore, O ye kings: be instructed, ye judges of the earth. 2:11 Serve the LORD with fear, and rejoice with trembling. 2:12 Kiss the Son, lest he be angry, and ye perish from the way, when his wrath is kindled but a little. Blessed are all they that put their trust in him.

3

Lord, how are they increased that trouble me! many are they that rise up against me. 3:2 Many there be which say of my soul, There is no help for him in God. Selah. 3:3 But thou, O

LORD, art a shield for me; my glory, and the lifter up of mine head. 3:4 I cried unto the **LORD** with my voice, and he heard me out of his holy hill. Selah. 3:5 I laid me down and slept; I awaked; for the **LORD** sustained me. 3:6 I will not be afraid of ten thousands of people, that have set themselves against me round about. 3:7 Arise, **O LORD**; save me, **O my God**: for thou hast smitten all mine enemies upon the cheek bone; thou hast broken the teeth of the ungodly. 3:8 Salvation belongeth unto the **LORD**: thy blessing is upon thy people. Selah.

4

Hear me when I call, **O God** of my righteousness: thou hast enlarged me when I was in distress; have mercy upon me, and hear my prayer. 4:2 O ye sons of men, how long will ye turn my glory into shame? how long will ye love vanity, and seek after leasing? Selah. 4:3 But know that the **LORD** hath set apart him that is godly for himself: the **LORD** will hear when I call unto him. 4:4 Stand in awe, and sin not: commune with your own heart upon your bed, and be still. Selah. 4:5

Offer the sacrifices of righteousness, and put your trust in the **LORD**. 4:6 **T**here be many that say, Who will shew us any good? **LORD**, lift thou up the light of thy countenance upon us. 4:7 **T**hou hast put gladness in my heart, more than in the time that their corn and their wine increased. 4:8 **I** will both lay me down in peace, and sleep: for thou, **LORD**, only makest me dwell in safety.

5

Give ear to my words, **O LORD**, consider my meditation. 5:2 **H**earken unto the voice of my cry, my King, and my God: for unto thee will I pray. 5:3 **M**y voice shalt thou hear in the morning, **O LORD**; in the morning will I direct my prayer unto thee, and will look up. 5:4 **F**or thou art not a God that hath pleasure in wickedness: neither shall evil dwell with thee. 5:5 **T**he foolish shall not stand in thy sight: thou hatest all workers of iniquity. 5:6 **T**hou shalt destroy them that speak leasing: the **LORD** will abhor the bloody and deceitful man. 5:7 **B**ut as for me, I will come into thy house in the multitude of thy mercy: and in thy fear will I worship toward thy holy temple. 5:8 Lead me, **O LORD**, in thy righteousness because of mine enemies; make thy way straight before my face. 5:9 For there is no faithfulness in their mouth; their inward part is very wickedness; their throat is an open sepulchre; they flatter with their tongue. 5:10 Destroy thou them, **O God**; let them fall by their own counsels; cast them out in the multitude of their transgressions; for they have rebelled against thee. 5:11 But let all those that put their trust in thee rejoice: let them ever shout for joy, because thou defendest them: let them also that love thy name be joyful in thee. 5:12 For thou, **LORD**, wilt bless the righteous; with favour wilt thou compass him as with a shield.

6

O LORD, rebuke me not in thine anger, neither chasten me in thy hot displeasure. 6:2 Have mercy upon me, **O LORD**; for I am weak: **O LORD**, heal me; for my bones are vexed. 6:3 My soul is also sore vexed: but thou, **O LORD**, how long? 6:4 Return, **O LORD**, deliver my soul: oh save me for thy mercies' sake. 6:5

For in death there is no remembrance of thee: in the grave who shall give thee thanks? 6:6 I am weary with my groaning; all the night make I my bed to swim; I water my couch with my tears. 6:7 Mine eye is consumed because of grief; it waxeth old because of all mine enemies. 6:8 Depart from me, all ye workers of iniquity; for the LORD hath heard the voice of my weeping. 6:9 The LORD hath heard my supplication; the LORD will receive my prayer. 6:10 Let all mine enemies be ashamed and sore vexed: let them return and be ashamed suddenly.

7

O LORD my God, in thee do I put my trust: save me from all them that persecute me, and deliver me: 7:2 Lest he tear my soul like a lion, rending it in pieces, while there is none to deliver. 7:3 O LORD my God, if I have done this; if there be iniquity in my hands; 7:4 If I have rewarded evil unto him that was at peace with me; (yea, I have delivered him that without cause is mine enemy:) 7:5 Let the enemy persecute my soul, and take it; yea, let him tread down my life upon the earth, and lay mine honour in the dust. Selah. **7:6** Arise, **O LORD**, in thine anger, lift up thyself because of the rage of mine enemies: and awake for me to the judgment that thou hast commanded. **7:7** So shall the congregation of the people compass thee about: for their sakes therefore return thou on high. **7:8** The **LORD** shall judge the people: judge me, **O LORD**, according to my righteousness, and according to mine integrity that is in me. **7:9** Oh let the wickedness of the wicked come to an end; but establish the just: for the righteous God trieth the hearts and reins. **7:10** My defence is of God, which saveth the upright in heart. **7:11** God judgeth the righteous, and God is angry with the wicked every day. **7:12** If he turn not, he will whet his sword; he hath bent his bow, and made it ready. **7:13** He hath also prepared for him the instruments of death; he ordaineth his arrows against the persecutors. **7:14** Behold, he travaileth with iniquity, and hath conceived mischief, and brought forth falsehood. **7:15** He made a pit, and digged it, and is fallen into the ditch which he made. **7:16** His mischief shall return upon his own head, and his violent dealing shall come down upon his own pate. **7:17** I will praise the **LORD** according to his righteousness: and will sing praise to the name of the **LORD** most high.

O LORD, our Lord, how excellent is thy name in all the earth! who hast set thy glory above the heavens. 8:2 Out of the mouth of babes and sucklings hast thou ordained strength because of thine enemies, that thou mightest still the enemy and the avenger. 8:3 When I consider thy heavens, the work of thy fingers, the moon and the stars, which thou hast ordained; 8:4 What is man, that thou art mindful of him? and the son of man, that thou visitest him? 8:5 For thou hast made him a little lower than the angels, and hast crowned him with glory and honour. 8:6 Thou madest him to have dominion over the works of thy hands; thou hast put all things under his feet: 8:7 All sheep and oxen, yea, and the beasts of the field; 8:8 The fowl of the air, and the fish of the sea, and whatsoever passeth through the paths of the seas. 8:9 O LORD our Lord, how excellent is thy name in all the earth!

9

I will praise thee, **O LORD**, with my whole heart; I will shew forth all thy marvellous works. 9:2 I will be glad and rejoice in thee: I will sing praise to thy name, **O** thou most **High**. 9:3 When mine enemies are turned back, they shall fall and perish at thy presence. 9:4 For thou hast maintained my right and my cause; thou satest in the throne judging right. 9:5 Thou hast rebuked the heathen, thou hast destroyed the wicked, thou hast put out their name for ever and ever. 9:6 O thou enemy, destructions are come to a perpetual end: and thou hast destroyed cities; their memorial is perished with them. 9:7 But the **LORD** shall endure for ever: he hath prepared his throne for judgment. 9:8 And he shall judge the world in righteousness, he shall minister judgment to the people in uprightness. 9:9 The **LORD** also will be a refuge for the oppressed, a refuge in times of trouble. 9:10 And they that know thy name will put their trust in thee: for thou, **LORD**, hast not forsaken them that seek thee. 9:11 Sing praises to the **LORD**, which dwelleth in Zion: declare among the people his doings. 9:12 When he maketh inquisition for blood, he remembereth them: he forgetteth not the cry of the humble. 9:13 Have mercy upon me, **O LORD**; consider my trouble which I suffer of them that hate me, thou that liftest me up from the gates of death: 9:14 That I may shew forth all thy praise in the gates of the daughter of Zion: I will rejoice in thy salvation. 9:15 The heathen are sunk down in the pit that they made: in the net which they hid is their own foot taken. 9:16 The **LORD** is known by the judgment which he executeth: the wicked is snared in the work of his own hands. Higgaion. Selah. 9:17 The wicked shall be turned into hell, and all the nations that forget God. 9:18 For the needy shall not alway be forgotten: the expectation of the poor shall not perish for ever. 9:19 Arise, **O LORD**; let not man prevail: let the heathen be judged in thy sight. 9:20 Put them in fear, **O LORD**: that the nations may know themselves to be but men. Selah.

10

Why standest thou afar off, **O LORD**? why hidest thou thyself in times of trouble? 10:2 The wicked in his pride doth persecute the poor: let them be taken in the devices that they have imagined. 10:3 For the wicked boasteth of his heart's desire, and blesseth the covetous, whom the

LORD abhorreth. 10:4 The wicked, through the pride of his countenance, will not seek after God: God is not in all his thoughts. 10:5 His ways are always grievous; thy judgments are far above out of his sight: as for all his enemies, he puffeth at them. 10:6 He hath said in his heart, I shall not be moved: for I shall never be in adversity. 10:7 His mouth is full of cursing and deceit and fraud: under his tongue is mischief and vanity. 10:8 He sitteth in the lurking places of the villages: in the secret places doth he murder the innocent: his eyes are privily set against the poor. 10:9 He lieth in wait secretly as a lion in his den: he lieth in wait to catch the poor: he doth catch the poor, when he draweth him into his net. 10:10 He croucheth, and humbleth himself, that the poor may fall by his strong ones. 10:11 He hath said in his heart, God hath forgotten: he hideth his face; he will never see it. 10:12 Arise, **O LORD**; **O God**, lift up thine hand: forget not the humble. 10:13 Wherefore doth the wicked contemn God? he hath said in his heart, Thou wilt not require it. 10:14 Thou hast seen it; for thou beholdest mischief and spite, to requite it with thy hand: the poor committeth himself unto thee; thou art the helper of the fatherless. 10:15 Break thou the arm of the wicked and the evil man: seek out his wickedness till thou find none. 10:16 The **LORD** is King for ever and ever: the heathen are perished out of his land. 10:17 **LORD**, thou hast heard the desire of the humble: thou wilt prepare their heart, thou wilt cause thine ear to hear:  10:18 To judge the fatherless and the oppressed, that the man of the earth may no more oppress.

11

In the **LORD** put I my trust: how say ye to my soul, Flee as a bird to your mountain? 11:2 For, lo, the wicked bend their bow, they make ready their arrow upon the string, that they may privily shoot at the upright in heart. 11:3 If the foundations be destroyed, what can the righteous do? 11:4 The **LORD** is in his holy temple, the **LORD**'s throne is in heaven: his eyes behold, his eyelids try, the children of men. 11:5 The **LORD** trieth the righteous: but the wicked and him that loveth violence his soul hateth. 11:6 Upon the wicked he shall rain snares, fire and brimstone, and an horrible tempest: this shall be the portion of their cup. 11:7 For the righteous **LORD** loveth righteousness; his countenance doth behold the upright.

12

Help, **LORD**; for the godly man ceaseth; for the faithful fail from among the children of men. 12:2 They speak vanity every one with his neighbour: with flattering lips and with a double heart do they speak. 12:3 The **LORD** shall cut off all flattering lips, and the tongue that speaketh proud things: 12:4 Who have said, With our tongue will we prevail; our lips are our own: who is lord over us? 12:5 For the oppression of the poor, for the sighing of the needy, now will I arise, saith the **LORD**; I will set him in safety from him that puffeth at him. 12:6 The words of the **LORD** are pure words: as silver tried in a furnace of earth, purified seven times. 12:7 Thou shalt keep them, **O LORD**, thou shalt preserve them from this generation for ever. 12:8 The wicked walk on every side, when the vilest men are exalted.

13

How long wilt thou forget me, **O LORD**? for ever? how long wilt thou hide thy face from me? 13:2 How long shall I take counsel in my soul, having sorrow in my heart daily? how long shall mine enemy be exalted over me? 13:3 Consider and hear me, **O LORD** my God: lighten mine eyes, lest I sleep the sleep of death; 13:4 Lest mine enemy say, I have prevailed against him; and those that trouble me rejoice when I am moved. 13:5 But I have trusted in thy mercy; my heart shall rejoice in thy salvation. 13:6 I will sing unto the **LORD**, because he hath dealt bountifully with me.

14

The fool hath said in his heart, There is no God. They are corrupt, they have done abominable works, there is none that doeth good. 14:2 The **LORD** looked down from heaven upon the children of men, to see if there were any that did understand, and seek God. 14:3 They are all gone aside, they are all together become filthy:

there is none that doeth good, no, not one. 14:4 Have all the workers of iniquity no knowledge? who eat up my people as they eat bread, and call not upon the LORD. 14:5 There were they in great fear: for God is in the generation of the righteous. 14:6 Ye have shamed the counsel of the poor, because the LORD is his refuge. 14:7 Oh that the salvation of Israel were come out of Zion! when the LORD bringeth back the captivity of his people, Jacob shall rejoice, and Israel shall be glad.

15

Lord, who shall abide in thy tabernacle? who shall dwell in thy holy hill? 15:2 He that walketh uprightly, and worketh righteousness, and speaketh the truth in his heart. 15:3 He that backbiteth not with his tongue, nor doeth evil to his neighbour, nor taketh up a reproach against his neighbour. 15:4 In whose eyes a vile person is contemned; but he honoureth them that fear the LORD. He that sweareth to his own hurt, and changeth not. 15:5 He that putteth not out his money to usury, nor taketh reward against the innocent. He that doeth these things shall never be moved.

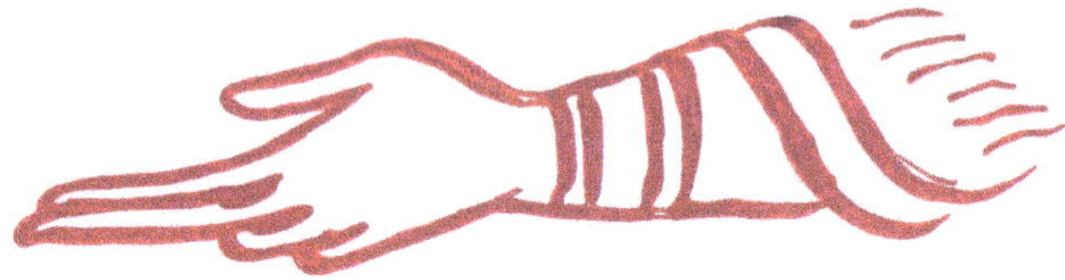

16

Preserve me, **O God**: for in thee do **I** put my trust. **16:2** **O** my soul, thou hast said unto the **LORD**, Thou art my Lord: my goodness extendeth not to thee; **16:3** **B**ut to the saints that are in the earth, and to the excellent, in whom is all my delight. **16:4** **T**heir sorrows shall be multiplied that hasten after another god: their drink offerings of blood will **I** not offer, nor take up their names into my lips. **16:5** **T**he **LORD** is the portion of mine inheritance and of my cup: thou maintainest my lot. **16:6** **T**he lines are fallen unto me in pleasant places; yea, **I** have a goodly heritage. **16:7** **I** will bless the **LORD**, who hath given me counsel: my reins also instruct me in the night seasons. **16:8** **I** have set the **LORD** always before me: because he is at my right hand, **I** shall not be moved. **16:9** **T**herefore my heart is glad, and my glory rejoiceth: my flesh also shall rest in hope. **16:10** **F**or thou wilt not leave my soul in hell; neither wilt thou suffer thine **Holy One** to see corruption. 16:11 **T**hou wilt shew me the path of life: in thy presence is fulness of joy; at thy right hand there are pleasures for evermore.

17

Hear the right, **O LORD**, attend unto my cry, give ear unto my prayer, that goeth not out of feigned lips. 17:2 **L**et my sentence come forth from thy presence; let thine eyes behold the things that are equal. 17:3 **T**hou hast proved mine heart; thou hast visited me in the night; thou hast tried me, and shalt find nothing; I am purposed that my mouth shall not transgress. 17:4 **C**oncerning the works of men, by the word of thy lips I have kept me from the paths of the destroyer. 17:5 **H**old up my goings in thy paths, that my footsteps slip not. 17:6 **I** have called upon thee, for thou wilt hear me, **O** God: incline thine ear unto me, and hear my speech. 17:7 **S**hew thy marvellous lovingkindness, **O** thou that savest by thy right hand them which put their trust in thee from those that rise up against them. 17:8 **K**eep me as the apple of the eye, hide me under the shadow of thy wings, 17:9 **F**rom the wicked that oppress me, from my deadly enemies, who compass me about. 17:10 They are inclosed in their own fat: with their mouth they speak proudly. 17:11 They have now compassed us in our steps: they have set their eyes bowing down to the earth; 17:12 Like as a lion that is greedy of his prey, and as it were a young lion lurking in secret places. 17:13 Arise, **O LORD**, disappoint him, cast him down: deliver my soul from the wicked, which is thy sword: 17:14 From men which are thy hand, **O LORD**, from men of the world, which have their portion in this life, and whose belly thou fillest with thy hid treasure: they are full of children, and leave the rest of their substance to their babes. 17:15 As for me, I will behold thy face in righteousness: I shall be satisfied, when I awake, with thy likeness.

18

I will love thee, **O LORD**, my strength. 18:2 The **LORD** is my rock, and my fortress, and my deliverer; my God, my strength, in whom I will trust; my buckler, and the horn of my salvation, and my high tower. 18:3 I will call upon the **LORD**, who is worthy to be praised: so shall I be saved from mine enemies. 18:4 The sorrows of death compassed me, and the floods of ungodly men made me afraid. 18:5 The sorrows of hell compassed me about: the snares of death prevented me. 18:6 In my distress I called upon the **LORD**, and cried unto my God: he heard my voice out of his temple, and my cry came before him, even into his ears. 18:7 Then the earth shook and trembled; the foundations also of the hills moved and were shaken, because he was wroth. 18:8 There went up a smoke out of his nostrils, and fire out of his mouth devoured: coals were kindled by it. 18:9 He bowed the heavens also, and came down: and darkness was under his feet. 18:10 And he rode upon a cherub, and did fly: yea, he did fly upon the wings of the wind. 18:11 He made darkness his secret place; his pavilion round about him were dark waters and thick clouds of the skies. 18:12 At the brightness that was before him his thick clouds passed, hail stones and coals of fire. 18:13 The **LORD** also thundered in the heavens, and the Highest gave his voice; hail stones and coals of fire. 18:14 Yea, he sent out his arrows, and scattered them; and he shot out lightnings, and discomfited them. 18:15 Then the channels of waters were seen, and the foundations of the world were discovered at thy rebuke, **O LORD**, at the blast of the breath of thy nostrils. 18:16 He sent from above, he took me, he drew me out of many waters. 18:17 He delivered me from my strong enemy, and from them which hated me: for they were too strong for me. 18:18 They prevented me in the day of my calamity: but the **LORD** was my stay. 18:19 He brought me forth also into a large place; he delivered me, because he delighted in me. 18:20 The **LORD** rewarded me according to my righteousness; according to the cleanness of my hands hath he recompensed me. 18:21 For I have kept the ways of the **LORD**, and have not wickedly departed from my God. 18:22 For all his judgments were before me, and I did not put away his statutes from me. 18:23 I was also upright before him, and I kept myself from mine iniquity. 18:24 Therefore hath the **LORD** recompensed me according to my righteousness, according to the cleanness of my hands in his eyesight. 18:25 With the merciful thou wilt shew thyself merciful; with an upright man thou wilt shew thyself upright; 18:26 With the pure thou wilt shew thyself pure; and with the froward thou wilt shew thyself froward. 18:27 For thou wilt save the afflicted people; but wilt bring down high looks. 18:28 For thou wilt light my candle: the **LORD** my God will enlighten my darkness. 18:29 For by thee I have run through a troop; and by my God have I leaped over a wall. 18:30 As for God, his way is perfect: the word of the **LORD** is tried: he is a buckler to all those that trust in him. 18:31

For who is God save the LORD? or who is a rock save our God? 18:32 It is God that girdeth me with strength, and maketh my way perfect. 18:33 He maketh my feet like hinds' feet, and setteth me upon my high places. 18:34 He teacheth my hands to war, so that a bow of steel is broken by mine arms. 18:35 Thou hast also given me the shield of thy salvation: and thy right hand hath holden me up, and thy gentleness hath made me great. 18:36 Thou hast enlarged my steps under me, that my feet did not slip. 18:37 I have pursued mine enemies, and overtaken them: neither did I turn again till they were consumed. 18:38 I have wounded them that they were not able to rise: they are fallen under my feet. 18:39 For thou hast girded me with strength unto the battle: thou hast subdued under me those that rose up against me. 18:40 Thou hast also given me the necks of mine enemies; that I might destroy them that hate me. 18:41 They cried, but there was none to save them: even unto the LORD, but he answered them not. 18:42 Then did I beat them small as the dust before the wind: I did cast them out as the dirt in the streets. 18:43 Thou hast delivered me from the strivings of the people; and thou hast made me the head of the heathen: a people whom I have not known shall serve me. 18:44 As soon as they hear of me, they shall obey me: the strangers shall submit themselves unto me. 18:45 The strangers shall fade away, and be afraid out of their close places. 18:46 The **LORD** liveth; and blessed be my rock; and let the God of my salvation be exalted. 18:47 It is God that avengeth me, and subdueth the people under me. 18:48 He delivereth me from mine enemies: yea, thou liftest me up above those that rise up against me: thou hast delivered me from the violent man. 18:49 Therefore will I give thanks unto thee, **O LORD**, among the heathen, and sing praises unto thy name. 18:50 Great deliverance giveth he to his king; and sheweth mercy to his anointed, to David, and to his seed for evermore.

19

The heavens declare the glory of God; and the firmament sheweth his handywork. 19:2 Day unto day uttereth speech, and night unto night sheweth knowledge. 19:3 There is no speech nor language, where their voice is not heard. 19:4 Their line is gone out through all the earth, and their words to the end of the world. In them hath he set a tabernacle for the sun, 19:5 Which is as a bridegroom coming out of his chamber, and rejoiceth as a strong man to run a race. 19:6 His going forth is from the end of the heaven, and his circuit unto the ends of it: and there is nothing hid from the heat thereof. 19:7 The law of the **LORD** is perfect, converting the soul: the testimony of the **LORD** is sure, making wise the simple. 19:8 The statutes of the **LORD** are right, rejoicing the heart: the commandment of the **LORD** is pure, enlightening the eyes. 19:9 The fear of the **LORD** is clean, enduring for ever: the judgments of the **LORD** are true and righteous altogether. 19:10 More to be desired are they than gold, yea, than much fine gold: sweeter also than honey and the honeycomb. 19:11 Moreover by them is thy servant warned: and in keeping of them there is great reward. 19:12 Who can understand his errors? cleanse thou me from secret faults. 19:13 Keep back thy servant also from presumptuous sins; let them not have dominion over me: then shall I be upright, and I shall be innocent from the great transgression. 19:14 Let the words of my mouth, and the meditation of my heart, be acceptable in thy sight, **O LORD**, my strength, and my redeemer.

20

The **LORD** hear thee in the day of trouble; the name of the God of Jacob defend thee; 20:2 Send thee help from the sanctuary, and strengthen thee out of Zion;  20:3 Remember all thy offerings, and accept thy burnt sacrifice; Selah. 20:4 Grant thee according to thine own heart, and fulfil all thy counsel. 20:5 We will rejoice in thy salvation, and in the name of our God we will set up our banners: the **LORD** fulfil all thy petitions. 20:6 Now know I that the **LORD** saveth his anointed; he will hear him from his holy heaven with the saving strength of his right hand. 20:7 Some trust in chariots, and some in horses: but we will remember the name of the **LORD** our God. 20:8 They are brought down and fallen: but we are risen, and stand upright. 20:9 Save, **LORD**: let the king hear us when we call.

21

The king shall joy in thy strength, **O LORD**; and in thy salvation how greatly shall he rejoice! 21:2 Thou hast given him his heart's desire, and hast not withholden the request of his lips. Selah. 21:3 For thou preventest him with the blessings of goodness: thou settest a crown of pure gold on his head. 21:4 He asked life of thee, and thou gavest it him, even length of days for ever and ever. 21:5 His glory is great in thy salvation: honour and majesty hast thou laid upon him. 21:6 For thou hast made him most blessed for ever: thou hast made him exceeding glad with thy countenance. 21:7 For the king trusteth in the **LORD**, and through the mercy of the most **High** he shall not be moved. 21:8 Thine hand shall find out all thine enemies: thy right hand shall find out those that hate thee. 21:9 Thou shalt make them as a fiery oven in the time of thine anger: the **LORD** shall swallow them up in his wrath, and the fire shall devour them. 21:10 Their fruit shalt thou destroy from the earth, and their seed from among the children of men. 21:11 For they intended evil against thee: they imagined a mischievous device, which they are not able to perform. 21:12 Therefore shalt thou make them turn their back, when thou shalt make ready thine arrows upon thy strings against the face of them. 21:13 Be thou exalted, **LORD**, in thine own strength: so will we sing and praise thy power.

My God, my God, why hast thou forsaken me? why art thou so far from helping me, and from the words of my roaring? 22:2 O my God, I cry in the day time, but thou hearest not; and in the night season, and am not silent. 22:3 But thou art holy, O thou that inhabitest the praises of Israel. 22:4 Our fathers trusted in thee: they trusted, and thou didst deliver them. 22:5 They cried unto thee, and were delivered: they trusted in thee, and were not confounded. 22:6 But I am a worm, and no man; a reproach of men, and despised of the people. 22:7 All they that see me laugh me to scorn: they shoot out the lip, they shake the head, saying, 22:8 He trusted on the LORD that he would deliver him: let him deliver him, seeing he delighted in him. 22:9 But thou art he that took me out of the womb: thou didst make me hope when I was upon my mother's breasts. 22:10 I was cast upon thee from the womb: thou art my God from my mother's belly. 22:11 Be not far from me; for trouble is near; for there is none to help. 22:12 Many bulls have compassed me: strong bulls of Bashan have beset me round. 22:13 They gaped upon me with their mouths, as a ravening and a roaring lion. 22:14 I am poured out like water, and all my bones are out of joint: my heart is like wax; it is melted in the midst of my bowels. 22:15 My strength is dried up like a potsherd; and my tongue cleaveth to my jaws; and thou hast brought me into the dust of death. 22:16 For dogs have compassed me: the assembly of the wicked have inclosed me: they pierced my hands and my feet. 22:17 I may tell all my bones: they look and stare upon me. 22:18 They part my garments among them, and cast lots upon my vesture. 22:19 But be not thou far from me, O LORD: O my strength, haste thee to help me. 22:20 Deliver my soul from the sword; my darling from the power of the dog. 22:21 Save me from the lion's mouth: for thou hast heard me from the horns of the unicorns. 22:22 I will declare thy name unto my brethren: in the midst of the congregation will I praise thee. 22:23 Ye that fear the LORD, praise him; all ye the seed of Jacob, glorify him; and fear him, all ye the seed of Israel. 22:24 For he hath not despised nor abhorred the affliction of the afflicted; neither hath he hid his face from him; but when he cried unto him, he heard. 22:25 My praise shall be of thee in the great congregation: I will pay my vows before them that fear him. 22:26 The meek shall eat and be satisfied: they shall praise the LORD that seek him: your heart shall live for ever. 22:27 All the ends of the world shall remember and turn unto the LORD: and all the kindreds of the nations shall worship before thee. 22:28 For the kingdom is the LORD's: and he is the governor among the nations.

22:29 All they that be fat upon earth shall eat and worship: all they that go down to the dust shall bow before him: and none can keep alive his own soul. 22:30 A seed shall serve him; it shall be accounted to the Lord for a generation. 22:31 They shall come, and shall declare his righteousness unto a people that shall be born, that he hath done this.

23

The **LORD** is my shepherd; I shall not want. 23:2 He maketh me to lie down in green pastures: he leadeth me beside the still waters. 23:3 He restoreth my soul: he leadeth me in the paths of righteousness for his name's sake. 23:4 Yea, though I walk through the valley of the shadow of death, I will fear no evil: for thou art with me; thy rod and thy staff they comfort me. 23:5 Thou preparest a table before me in the presence of mine enemies: thou anointest my head with oil; my cup runneth over. 23:6 Surely goodness and mercy shall follow me all the days of my life: and I will dwell in the house of the **LORD** for ever.

24

The earth is the **LORD**'s, and the fulness thereof; the world, and they that dwell therein. 24:2 For he hath founded it upon the seas, and established it upon the floods. 24:3 Who shall ascend into the hill of the **LORD**? or who shall stand in his holy place? 24:4 He that hath clean hands, and a pure heart; who hath not lifted up his soul unto vanity, nor sworn deceitfully. 24:5 He shall receive the blessing from the **LORD**, and righteousness from the God of his salvation. 24:6 This is the generation of them that seek him, that seek thy face, **O** Jacob. Selah. 24:7 Lift up your heads, **O** ye gates; and be ye lift up, ye everlasting doors; and the King of glory shall come in. 24:8 Who is this King of glory? The **LORD** strong and mighty, the **LORD** mighty in battle. 24:9 Lift up your heads, **O** ye gates; even lift them up, ye everlasting doors; and the King of glory shall come in. 24:10 Who is this King of glory? The **LORD** of hosts, he is the King of glory. Selah.

Unto thee, **O LORD**, do I lift up my soul. 25:2 O my God, I trust in thee: let me not be ashamed, let not mine enemies triumph over me. 25:3 Yea, let none that wait on thee be ashamed: let them be ashamed which transgress without cause. 25:4 Shew me thy ways, **O LORD**; teach me thy paths. 25:5 Lead me in thy truth, and teach me: for thou art the God of my salvation; on thee do I wait all the day. 25:6 Remember, **O LORD**, thy tender mercies and thy lovingkindnesses; for they have been ever of old. 25:7 Remember not the sins of my youth, nor my transgressions: according to thy mercy remember thou me for thy goodness' sake, **O LORD**. 25:8 Good and upright is the **LORD**: therefore will he teach sinners in the way. 25:9 The meek will he guide in judgment: and the meek will he teach his way. 25:10 All the paths of the **LORD** are mercy and truth unto such as keep his covenant and his testimonies. 25:11 For thy name's sake, **O LORD**, pardon mine iniquity; for it is great. 25:12 What man is he that feareth the **LORD**? him shall he teach in the way that he shall choose. 25:13 His soul shall dwell at ease; and his seed shall inherit the earth. 25:14 The secret of the **LORD** is with them that fear him; and he will shew them his covenant. 25:15 Mine eyes are ever toward the **LORD**; for he shall pluck my feet out of the net. 25:16 Turn thee unto me, and have mercy upon me; for I am desolate and afflicted. 25:17 The troubles of my heart are enlarged: O bring thou me out of my distresses. 25:18 Look upon mine affliction and my pain; and forgive all my sins. 25:19 Consider mine enemies; for they are many; and they hate me with cruel hatred. 25:20 O keep my soul, and deliver me: let me not be ashamed; for I put my trust in thee. 25:21 Let integrity and uprightness preserve me; for I wait on thee. 25:22 Redeem Israel, O God, out of all his troubles.

26

Judge me, O LORD; for I have walked in mine integrity: I have trusted also in the LORD; therefore I shall not slide. 26:2 Examine me, O LORD, and prove me; try my reins and my heart. 26:3 For thy lovingkindness is before mine eyes: and I have walked in thy truth. 26:4 I have not sat with vain persons, neither will I go in with dissemblers. 26:5 I have hated the congregation of evil doers; and will not sit with the wicked.

26:6 **I** will wash mine hands in innocency: so will I compass thine altar, **O LORD**: 26:7 **T**hat I may publish with the voice of thanksgiving, and tell of all thy wondrous works. 26:8 **LORD**, I have loved the habitation of thy house, and the place where thine honour dwelleth. 26:9 **G**ather not my soul with sinners, nor my life with bloody men: 26:10 **I**n whose hands is mischief, and their right hand is full of bribes. 26:11 **B**ut as for me, I will walk in mine integrity: redeem me, and be merciful unto me. 26:12 **M**y foot standeth in an even place: in the congregations will I bless the **LORD**.

27

The **LORD** is my light and my salvation; whom shall I fear? the **LORD** is the strength of my life; of whom shall I be afraid? 27:2 **W**hen the wicked, even mine enemies and my foes, came upon me to eat up my flesh, they stumbled and fell. 27:3 **T**hough an host should encamp against me, my heart shall not fear: though war should rise against me, in this will I be confident. 27:4 **O**ne thing have

I desired of the **LORD**, that will I seek after; that I may dwell in the house of the **LORD** all the days of my life, to behold the beauty of the **LORD**, and to enquire in his temple. 27:5 For in the time of trouble he shall hide me in his pavilion: in the secret of his tabernacle shall he hide me; he shall set me up upon a rock. 27:6 And now shall mine head be lifted up above mine enemies round about me: therefore will I offer in his tabernacle sacrifices of joy; I will sing, yea, I will sing praises unto the **LORD**. 27:7 Hear, **O LORD**, when I cry with my voice: have mercy also upon me, and answer me. 27:8 When thou saidst, Seek ye my face; my heart said unto thee, Thy face, **LORD**, will I seek. 27:9 Hide not thy face far from me; put not thy servant away in anger: thou hast been my help; leave me not, neither forsake me, **O God** of my salvation. 27:10 When my father and my mother forsake me, then the **LORD** will take me up. 27:11 Teach me thy way, **O LORD**, and lead me in a plain path, because of mine enemies. 27:12 Deliver me not over unto the will of mine enemies: for false witnesses are risen up against me, and such as breathe out cruelty. 27:13 I had fainted, unless I had believed to see the goodness of the **LORD** in the land of the living. 27:14 Wait on the **LORD**: be of good courage, and he shall strengthen thine heart: wait, I say, on the **LORD**.

Unto thee will I cry, **O LORD** my rock; be not silent to me: lest, if thou be silent to me, I become like them that go down into the pit. 28:2 **H**ear the voice of my supplications, when I cry unto thee, when I lift up my hands toward thy holy oracle. 28:3 **D**raw me not away with the wicked, and with the workers of iniquity, which speak peace to their neighbours, but mischief is in their hearts. 28:4 **G**ive them according to their deeds, and according to the wickedness of their endeavours: give them after the work of their hands; render to them their desert. 28:5 **B**ecause they regard not the works of the **LORD**, nor the operation of his hands, he shall destroy them, and not build them up. 28:6 **B**lessed be the **LORD**, because he hath heard the voice of my supplications. 28:7 **T**he **LORD** is my strength and my shield; my heart trusted in him, and I am helped: therefore my heart greatly rejoiceth; and with my song will I praise him. 28:8 **T**he **LORD** is their strength, and he is the saving strength of his anointed. 28:9 **S**ave thy people, and bless thine inheritance: feed them also, and lift them up for ever.

Give unto the **LORD**, **O** ye mighty, give unto the **LORD** glory and strength. 29:2 Give unto the **LORD** the glory due unto his name; worship the **LORD** in the beauty of holiness. 29:3 The voice of the **LORD** is upon the waters: the God of glory thundereth: the **LORD** is upon many waters. 29:4 The voice of the **LORD** is powerful; the voice of the **LORD** is full of majesty. 29:5 The voice of the **LORD** breaketh the cedars; yea, the **LORD** breaketh the cedars of Lebanon. 29:6 He maketh them also to skip like a calf; Lebanon and Sirion like a young unicorn. 29:7 The voice of the **LORD** divideth the flames of fire. 29:8 The voice of the **LORD** shaketh the wilderness; the **LORD** shaketh the wilderness of Kadesh. 29:9 The voice of the **LORD** maketh the hinds to calve, and discovereth the forests: and in his temple doth every one speak of his glory. 29:10 The **LORD** sitteth upon the flood; yea, the **LORD** sitteth King for ever. 29:11 The **LORD** will give strength unto his people; the **LORD** will bless his people with peace.

I will extol thee, **O LORD**; for thou hast lifted me up, and hast not made my foes to rejoice over me. 30:2 **O LORD** my God, I cried unto thee, and thou hast healed me. 30:3 **O LORD**, thou hast brought up my soul from the grave: thou hast kept me alive, that I should not go down to the pit. 30:4 Sing unto the **LORD**, **O** ye saints of his, and give thanks at the remembrance of his holiness. 30:5 For his anger endureth but a moment; in his favour is life: weeping may endure for a night, but joy cometh in the morning. 30:6 And in my prosperity I said, I shall never be moved. 30:7 **LORD**, by thy favour thou hast made my mountain to stand strong: thou didst hide thy face, and I was troubled. 30:8 I cried to thee, **O LORD**; and unto the **LORD** I made supplication. 30:9 What profit is there in my blood, when I go down to the pit? Shall the dust praise thee? shall it declare thy truth? 30:10 Hear, **O LORD**, and have mercy upon me: **LORD**, be thou my helper. 30:11 Thou hast turned for me my mourning into dancing: thou hast put off my sackcloth, and girded me with gladness; 30:12 To the end that my glory may sing praise to thee, and not be silent. **O LORD** my God, I will give thanks unto thee for ever.

In thee, **O LORD**, do I put my trust; let me never be ashamed: deliver me in thy righteousness. 31:2 Bow down thine ear to me; deliver me speedily: be thou my strong rock, for an house of defence to save me. 31:3 For thou art my rock and my fortress; therefore for thy name's sake lead me, and guide me. 31:4 Pull me out of the net that they have laid privily for me: for thou art my strength. 31:5 Into thine hand I commit my spirit: thou hast redeemed me, **O LORD** God of truth. 31:6 I have hated them that regard lying vanities: but I trust in the **LORD**. 31:7 I will be glad and rejoice in thy mercy: for thou hast considered my trouble; thou hast known my soul in adversities; 31:8 And hast not shut me up into the hand of the enemy: thou hast set my feet in a large room. 31:9 Have mercy upon me, **O LORD**, for I am in trouble: mine eye is consumed with grief, yea, my soul and my belly. 31:10 For my life is spent with grief, and my years with sighing: my strength faileth because of mine iniquity, and my bones are consumed. 31:11 I was a reproach among all mine enemies, but especially among my neighbours, and a fear to mine acquaintance: they that did see me without fled from me. 31:12 I am forgotten as a dead man out of mind: I am like a broken vessel. 31:13 For I have heard the slander of many: fear was on every side: while they took counsel together against me, they devised to take away my life. **31:14** But I trusted in thee, **O LORD**: I said, Thou art my God. **31:15** My times are in thy hand: deliver me from the hand of mine enemies, and from them that persecute me. **31:16** Make thy face to shine upon thy servant: save me for thy mercies' sake. **31:17** Let me not be ashamed, **O LORD**; for I have called upon thee: let the wicked be ashamed, and let them be silent in the grave. **31:18** Let the lying lips be put to silence; which speak grievous things proudly and contemptuously against the righteous. **31:19** Oh how great is thy goodness, which thou hast laid up for them that fear thee; which thou hast wrought for them that trust in thee before the sons of men! **31:20** Thou shalt hide them in the secret of thy presence from the pride of man: thou shalt keep them secretly in a pavilion from the strife of tongues. **31:21** Blessed be the **LORD**: for he hath shewed me his marvellous kindness in a strong city. **31:22** For I said in my haste, I am cut off from before thine eyes: nevertheless thou heardest the voice of my supplications when I cried unto thee. **31:23** O love the **LORD**, all ye his saints: for the **LORD** preserveth the faithful, and plentifully rewardeth the proud doer. **31:24** Be of good courage, and he shall strengthen your heart, all ye that hope in the **LORD**.

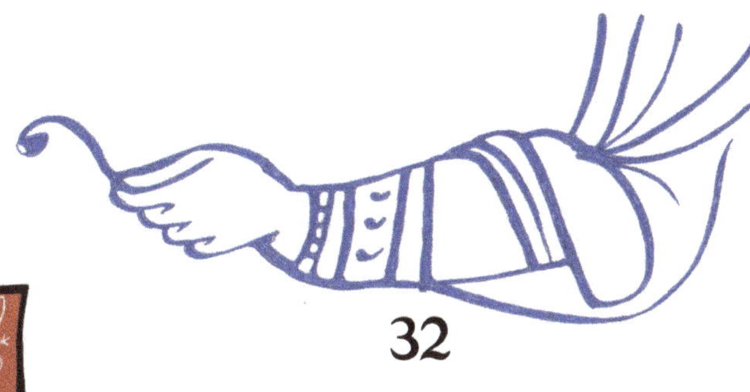

32

Blessed is he whose transgression is forgiven, whose sin is covered. 32:2 **B**lessed is the man unto whom the **LORD** imputeth not iniquity, and in whose spirit there is no guile. 32:3 **W**hen I kept silence, my bones waxed old through my roaring all the day long. 32:4 **F**or day and night thy hand was heavy upon me: my moisture is turned into the drought of summer. Selah. 32:5 **I** acknowledged my sin unto thee, and mine iniquity have I not hid. I said, I will confess my transgressions unto the **LORD**; and thou forgavest the iniquity of my sin. Selah. 32:6 **F**or this shall every one that is godly pray unto thee in a time when thou mayest be found: surely in the floods of great waters they shall not come nigh unto him. 32:7 **T**hou art my hiding place; thou shalt preserve me from trouble; thou shalt compass me about with songs of deliverance. Selah. 32:8 **I** will instruct thee and teach thee in the way which thou shalt go: I will guide thee with mine eye. 32:9 **B**e ye not as the horse, or as the mule, which have no understanding: whose mouth must be held in with bit and bridle, lest they come near unto thee.   32:10 Many sorrows shall be to the wicked: but he that trusteth in the **LORD**, mercy shall compass him about.   32:11 Be glad in the **LORD**, and rejoice, ye righteous: and shout for joy, all ye that are upright in heart.

33

Rejoice in the **LORD**, O ye righteous: for praise is comely for the upright.   33:2 Praise the **LORD** with harp: sing unto him with the psaltery and an instrument of ten strings.   33:3 Sing unto him a new song; play skilfully with a loud noise.   33:4 For the word of the **LORD** is right; and all his works are done in truth.   33:5 He loveth righteousness and judgment: the earth is full of the goodness of the **LORD**.   33:6 By the word of the **LORD** were the heavens made; and all the host of them by the breath of his mouth.   33:7 He gathereth the waters of the sea together as an heap: he layeth up the depth in storehouses.   33:8 Let all the earth fear the **LORD**: let all the inhabitants of the world stand in awe of him.   33:9 For he spake, and it was done; he commanded, and it stood fast. 33:10 The **LORD** bringeth the counsel of the heathen to nought: he maketh the devices of the people of none effect. 33:11 The counsel of the **LORD** standeth for ever, the thoughts of his heart to all generations. 33:12 Blessed is the nation whose God is the **LORD**; and the people whom he hath chosen for his own inheritance. 33:13 The **LORD** looketh from heaven; he beholdeth all the sons of men. 33:14 From the place of his habitation he looketh upon all the inhabitants of the earth. 33:15 He fashioneth their hearts alike; he considereth all their works. 33:16 There is no king saved by the multitude of an host: a mighty man is not delivered by much strength. 33:17 An horse is a vain thing for safety: neither shall he deliver any by his great strength. 33:18 Behold, the eye of the **LORD** is upon them that fear him, upon them that hope in his mercy; 33:19 To deliver their soul from death, and to keep them alive in famine. 33:20 Our soul waiteth for the **LORD**: he is our help and our shield. 33:21 For our heart shall rejoice in him, because we have trusted in his holy name. 33:22 Let thy mercy, **O LORD**, be upon us, according as we hope in thee.

I will bless the **LORD** at all times: his praise shall continually be in my mouth. 34:2 My soul shall make her boast in the **LORD**: the humble shall hear thereof, and be glad. 34:3 O magnify the **LORD** with me, and let us exalt his name together. 34:4 I sought the **LORD**, and he heard me, and delivered me from all my fears. 34:5 They looked unto him, and were lightened: and their faces were not ashamed. 34:6 This poor man cried, and the **LORD** heard him, and saved him out of all his troubles. 34:7 The angel of the **LORD** encampeth round about them that fear him, and delivereth them. 34:8 O taste and see that the **LORD** is good: blessed is the man that trusteth in him. 34:9 O fear the **LORD**, ye his saints: for there is no want to them that fear him. 34:10 The young lions do lack, and suffer hunger: but they that seek the **LORD** shall not want any good thing. 34:11 Come, ye children, hearken unto me: I will teach you the fear of the **LORD**. 34:12 What man is he that desireth life, and loveth many days, that he may see good? 34:13 Keep thy tongue from evil, and thy lips from speaking guile. 34:14 Depart from evil, and do good; seek peace, and pursue it. 34:15 The eyes of the **LORD** are upon the righteous, and his ears are open unto their cry. 34:16 The face of the **LORD** is against them that do evil, to cut off the remembrance of them from the earth. 34:17 The righteous cry, and the **LORD** heareth, and delivereth them out of all their troubles. 34:18 The **LORD** is nigh unto them that are of a broken heart; and saveth such as be of a contrite spirit. 34:19 Many are the afflictions of the righteous: but the **LORD** delivereth him out of them all. 34:20 He keepeth all his bones: not one of them is broken. 34:21 Evil shall slay the wicked: and they that hate the righteous shall be desolate. 34:22 The **LORD** redeemeth the soul of his servants: and none of them that trust in him shall be desolate.

35

Plead my cause, **O LORD**, with them that strive with me: fight against them that fight against me. 35:2 Take hold of shield and buckler, and stand up for mine help. 35:3 Draw out also the spear, and stop the way against them that persecute me: say unto my soul, I am thy salvation. 35:4 Let them be confounded and put to shame that seek after my soul: let them be turned back and brought to confusion that devise my hurt. 35:5 Let them be as chaff before the wind: and let the angel of the **LORD** chase them. 35:6 Let their way be dark and slippery: and let the angel of the **LORD** persecute them. 35:7 For without cause have they hid for me their net in a pit, which without cause they have digged for my soul. 35:8 Let destruction come upon him at unawares; and let his net that he hath hid catch himself: into that very destruction let him fall. 35:9 And my soul shall be joyful in the **LORD**: it shall rejoice in his salvation. 35:10 All my bones shall say, **LORD**, who is like unto thee, which deliverest the poor from him that is too strong for him, yea, the poor and the needy from him that spoileth him? 35:11 False witnesses did rise up; they laid to my charge things that I knew not. 35:12 They rewarded me evil for good to the spoiling of my soul. 35:13 But as for me, when they were sick, my clothing was sackcloth: I humbled my soul with fasting; and my prayer returned into mine own bosom. 35:14 I behaved myself as though he had been my friend or brother: I bowed down heavily, as one that mourneth for his mother. 35:15 But in mine adversity they rejoiced, and gathered themselves together: yea, the abjects gathered themselves together against me, and I knew it not; they did tear me, and ceased not: 35:16 With hypocritical mockers in feasts, they gnashed upon me with their teeth. 35:17 Lord, how long wilt thou look on? rescue my soul from their destructions, my darling from the lions. 35:18 I will give thee thanks in the great congregation: I will praise thee among much people. 35:19 Let not them that are mine enemies wrongfully rejoice over me: neither let them wink with the eye that hate me without a cause. 35:20 For they speak not peace: but they devise deceitful matters against them that are quiet in the land. 35:21 Yea, they opened their mouth wide against me, and said, Aha, aha, our eye hath seen it. 35:22 This thou hast seen, O LORD: keep not silence: O Lord, be not far from me. 35:23 Stir up thyself, and awake to my judgment, even unto my cause, my God and my Lord. 35:24 Judge me, O LORD my God, according to thy righteousness; and let them not rejoice over me. 35:25 Let them not say in their hearts, Ah, so would we have it: let them not say, We have swallowed him up. 35:26 Let them be ashamed and brought to confusion together that rejoice at mine hurt: let them be clothed with shame and dishonour that magnify themselves against me. 35:27 Let them shout for joy, and be glad, that favour my righteous cause: yea, let them say continually, Let the LORD be magnified, which hath pleasure in the prosperity of his servant. 35:28 And my tongue shall speak of thy righteousness and of thy praise all the day long.

The transgression of the wicked saith within my heart, that there is no fear of God before his eyes. 36:2 For he flattereth himself in his own eyes, until his iniquity be found to be hateful. 36:3 The words of his mouth are iniquity and deceit: he hath left off to be wise, and to do good. 36:4 He deviseth mischief upon his bed; he setteth himself in a way that is not good; he abhorreth not evil. 36:5 Thy mercy, O LORD, is in the heavens; and thy faithfulness reacheth unto the clouds. 36:6 Thy righteousness is like the great mountains; thy judgments are a great deep: O LORD, thou preservest man and beast. 36:7 How excellent is thy lovingkindness, O God! therefore the children of men put their trust under the shadow of thy wings. 36:8 They shall be abundantly satisfied with the fatness of thy house; and thou shalt make them drink of the river of thy pleasures. 36:9 For with thee is the fountain of life: in thy light shall we see light. 36:10 O continue thy lovingkindness unto them that know thee; and thy righteousness to the upright in heart. 36:11 Let not the foot of pride come against me, and let not the hand of the wicked remove me. 36:12 There are the workers of iniquity fallen: they are cast down, and shall not be able to rise.

37

Fret not thyself because of evildoers, neither be thou envious against the workers of iniquity. 37:2 For they shall soon be cut down like the grass, and wither as the green herb. 37:3 Trust in the **LORD**, and do good; so shalt thou dwell in the land, and verily thou shalt be fed. 37:4 Delight thyself also in the **LORD**: and he shall give thee the desires of thine heart. 37:5 Commit thy way unto the **LORD**; trust also in him; and he shall bring it to pass. 37:6 And he shall bring forth thy righteousness as the light, and thy judgment as the noonday. 37:7 Rest in the **LORD**, and wait patiently for him: fret not thyself because of him who prospereth in his way, because of the man who bringeth wicked devices to pass. 37:8 Cease from anger, and forsake wrath: fret not thyself in any wise to do evil. 37:9 For evildoers shall be cut off: but those that wait upon the **LORD**, they shall inherit the earth. 37:10 For yet a little while, and the wicked shall not be: yea, thou shalt diligently consider his place, and it shall not be. 37:11 But the meek shall inherit the earth; and shall delight themselves

in the abundance of peace. 37:12 The wicked
plotteth against the just, and gnasheth upon him
with his teeth. 37:13 The **LORD** shall laugh
at him: for he seeth that his day is coming. 37:14
The wicked have drawn out the sword, and have bent
their bow, to cast down the poor and needy, and to slay
such as be of upright conversation. 37:15 Their
sword shall enter into their own heart, and their bows
shall be broken. 37:16 A little that a righteous
man hath is better than the riches of many wicked.
37:17 For the arms of the wicked shall be broken:
but the **LORD** upholdeth the righteous. 37:18
The **LORD** knoweth the days of the upright: and their
inheritance shall be for ever. 37:19 They shall
not be ashamed in the evil time: and in the days of
famine they shall be satisfied. 37:20 But the
wicked shall perish, and the enemies of the **LORD** shall
be as the fat of lambs: they shall consume; into smoke
shall they consume away. 37:21 The wicked
borroweth, and payeth not again: but the righteous
sheweth mercy, and giveth. 37:22 For such as be
blessed of him shall inherit the earth; and they that
be cursed of him shall be cut off. 37:23 The
steps of a good man are ordered by the **LORD**: and
he delighteth in his way. 37:24 Though he
fall, he shall not be utterly cast down: for the **LORD**
upholdeth him with his hand. 37:25 I have been
young, and now am old; yet have I not seen the righteous
forsaken, nor his seed begging bread. 37:26 He

is ever merciful, and lendeth; and his seed is blessed. 37:27 Depart from evil, and do good; and dwell for evermore. 37:28 For the **LORD** loveth judgment, and forsaketh not his saints; they are preserved for ever: but the seed of the wicked shall be cut off. 37:29 The righteous shall inherit the land, and dwell therein for ever. 37:30 The mouth of the righteous speaketh wisdom, and his tongue talketh of judgment. 37:31 The law of his God is in his heart; none of his steps shall slide. 37:32 The wicked watcheth the righteous, and seeketh to slay him. 37:33 The **LORD** will not leave him in his hand, nor condemn him when he is judged. 37:34 Wait on the **LORD**, and keep his way, and he shall exalt thee to inherit the land: when the wicked are cut off, thou shalt see it. 37:35 I have seen the wicked in great power, and spreading himself like a green bay tree. 37:36 Yet he passed away, and, lo, he was not: yea, I sought him, but he could not be found. 37:37 Mark the perfect man, and behold the upright: for the end of that man is peace. 37:38 But the transgressors shall be destroyed together: the end of the wicked shall be cut off. 37:39 But the salvation of the righteous is of the **LORD**: he is their strength in the time of trouble. 37:40 And the **LORD** shall help them, and deliver them: he shall deliver them from the wicked, and save them, because they trust in him.

38

O LORD, rebuke me not in thy wrath: neither chasten me in thy hot displeasure. 38:2 For thine arrows stick fast in me, and thy hand presseth me sore. 38:3 There is no soundness in my flesh because of thine anger; neither is there any rest in my bones because of my sin. 38:4 For mine iniquities are gone over mine head: as an heavy burden they are too heavy for me. 38:5 My wounds stink and are corrupt because of my foolishness. 38:6 I am troubled; I am bowed down greatly; I go mourning all the day long. 38:7 For my loins are filled with a loathsome disease: and there is no soundness in my flesh. 38:8 I am feeble and sore broken: I have roared by reason of the disquietness of my heart. 38:9 Lord, all my desire is before thee; and my groaning is not hid from thee. 38:10 My heart panteth, my strength faileth me: as for the light of mine eyes, it also is gone from me. 38:11 My lovers and my friends stand aloof from my sore;

and my kinsmen stand afar off. 38:12 They
also that seek after my life lay snares for me: and
they that seek my hurt speak mischievous things, and
imagine deceits all the day long. 38:13 But I,
as a deaf man, heard not; and I was as a dumb man
that openeth not his mouth. 38:14 Thus I was
as a man that heareth not, and in whose mouth are
no reproofs. 38:15 For in thee, **O LORD**, do I hope:
thou wilt hear, **O Lord my God**. 38:16 For I
said, **Hear me**, lest otherwise they should rejoice over
me: when my foot slippeth, they magnify themselves
against me. 38:17 For I am ready to halt,
and my sorrow is continually before me. 38:18
For I will declare mine iniquity; I will be sorry for my
sin. 38:19 But mine enemies are lively, and
they are strong: and they that hate me wrongfully
are multiplied. 38:20 They also that render
evil for good are mine adversaries; because I follow the
thing that good is. 38:21 Forsake me not, **O
LORD**: **O my God**, be not far from me. 38:22 Make
haste to help me, **O Lord my salvation**.

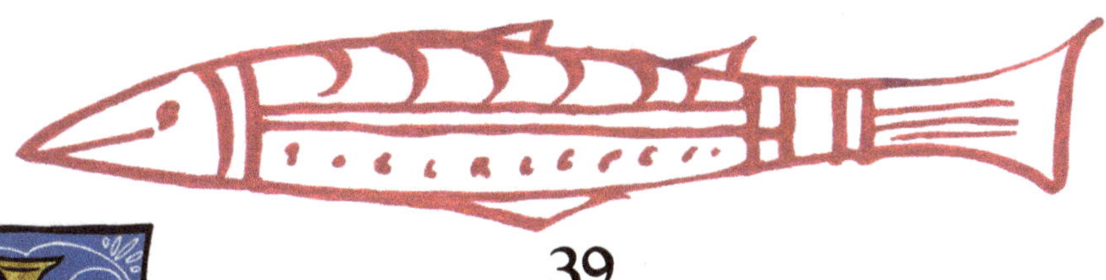

39

I said, I will take heed to my ways, that I sin
not with my tongue: I will keep my mouth

with a bridle, while the wicked is before me. 39:2 I was dumb with silence, I held my peace, even from good; and my sorrow was stirred. 39:3 My heart was hot within me, while I was musing the fire burned: then spake I with my tongue, 39:4 LORD, make me to know mine end, and the measure of my days, what it is: that I may know how frail I am. 39:5 Behold, thou hast made my days as an handbreadth; and mine age is as nothing before thee: verily every man at his best state is altogether vanity. Selah. 39:6 Surely every man walketh in a vain shew: surely they are disquieted in vain: he heapeth up riches, and knoweth not who shall gather them. 39:7 And now, Lord, what wait I for? my hope is in thee. 39:8 Deliver me from all my transgressions: make me not the reproach of the foolish. 39:9 I was dumb, I opened not my mouth; because thou didst it. 39:10 Remove thy stroke away from me: I am consumed by the blow of thine hand. 39:11 When thou with rebukes dost correct man for iniquity, thou makest his beauty to consume away like a moth: surely every man is vanity. Selah. 39:12 Hear my prayer, O LORD, and give ear unto my cry; hold not thy peace at my tears: for I am a stranger with thee, and a sojourner, as all my fathers were. 39:13 O spare me, that I may recover strength, before I go hence, and be no more.

40

I waited patiently for the **LORD**; and he inclined unto me, and heard my cry. 40:2 He brought me up also out of an horrible pit, out of the miry clay, and set my feet upon a rock, and established my goings. 40:3 And he hath put a new song in my mouth, even praise unto our God: many shall see it, and fear, and shall trust in the **LORD**. 40:4 Blessed is that man that maketh the **LORD** his trust, and respecteth not the proud, nor such as turn aside to lies. 40:5 Many, **O LORD** my God, are thy wonderful works which thou hast done, and thy thoughts which are to us-ward: they cannot be reckoned up in order unto thee: if I would declare and speak of them, they are more than can be numbered. 40:6 Sacrifice and offering thou didst not desire; mine ears hast thou opened: burnt offering and sin offering hast thou not required. 40:7 Then said I, Lo, I come: in the volume of the book it is written of me, 40:8 I delight to do thy will, **O my God**: yea, thy law is within my heart. 40:9 I have preached righteousness in the great congregation: lo, I have not refrained my lips, **O LORD**, thou knowest. 40:10 I have not hid thy righteousness within my heart; I have declared thy faithfulness and thy salvation: I have not concealed thy lovingkindness and thy truth from the great congregation. 40:11 Withhold not thou thy tender mercies from me, **O LORD**: let thy lovingkindness and thy truth continually preserve me. 40:12 For innumerable evils have compassed me about: mine iniquities have taken hold upon me, so that I am not able to look up; they are more than the hairs of mine head: therefore my heart faileth me. 40:13 Be pleased, **O LORD**, to deliver me: **O LORD**, make haste to help me. 40:14 Let them be ashamed and confounded together that seek after my soul to destroy it; let them be driven backward and put to shame that wish me evil. 40:15 Let them be desolate for a reward of their shame that say unto me, Aha, aha. 40:16 Let all those that seek thee rejoice and be glad in thee: let such as love thy salvation say continually, The **LORD** be magnified. 40:17 But I am poor and needy; yet the Lord thinketh upon me: thou art my help and my deliverer; make no tarrying, **O my God**.

Blessed is he that considereth the poor: the **LORD** will deliver him in time of trouble. 41:2 The **LORD** will preserve him, and keep him alive; and he shall be blessed upon the earth: and thou wilt not deliver him unto the will of his enemies. 41:3 The **LORD** will strengthen him upon the bed of languishing: thou wilt make all his bed in his sickness. 41:4 I said, **LORD**, be merciful unto me: heal my soul; for I have sinned against thee. 41:5 Mine enemies speak evil of me, When shall he die, and his name perish? 41:6 And if he come to see me, he speaketh vanity: his heart gathereth iniquity to itself; when he goeth abroad, he telleth it. 41:7 All that hate me whisper together against me: against me do they devise my hurt. 41:8 An evil disease, say they, cleaveth fast unto him: and now that he lieth he shall rise up no more. 41:9 Yea, mine own familiar friend, in whom I trusted, which did eat of my bread, hath lifted up his heel against me. 41:10 But thou, **O LORD**, be merciful unto me, and raise me up, that I may requite them. 41:11 By this I know that thou favourest me, because mine enemy doth not triumph over me. 41:12 And as for me, thou upholdest me in mine integrity, and settest me before thy face for ever. 41:13 Blessed be the **LORD** God of

Israel from everlasting, and to everlasting. Amen, and Amen.

42

As the hart panteth after the water brooks, so panteth my soul after thee, O God. 42:2 My soul thirsteth for God, for the living God: when shall I come and appear before God? 42:3 My tears have been my meat day and night, while they continually say unto me, Where is thy God? 42:4 When I remember these things, I pour out my soul in me: for I had gone with the multitude, I went with them to the house of God, with the voice of joy and praise, with a multitude that kept holyday. 42:5 Why art thou cast down, O my soul? and why art thou disquieted in me? hope thou in God: for I shall yet praise him for the help of his countenance. 42:6 O my God, my soul is cast down within me: therefore will I remember thee from the land of Jordan, and of the Hermonites, from the hill Mizar. 42:7 Deep calleth unto deep at the noise of thy waterspouts: all thy waves and thy billows are gone over me. 42:8 Yet the LORD will command his lovingkindness in the day time, and in the night his song shall be with me, and my prayer unto the God of my life. 42:9 I will say unto God my rock, Why hast thou forgotten me? why go I mourning because of the oppression of the enemy? 42:10 As with a sword in my bones, mine enemies reproach me; while they say daily unto me, Where is thy God? 42:11 Why art thou cast down, O my soul? and why art thou disquieted within me? hope thou in God: for I shall yet praise him, who is the health of my countenance, and my God.

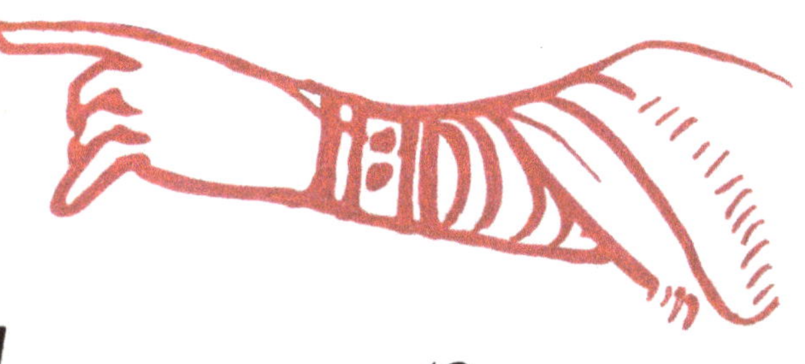

43

Judge me, O God, and plead my cause against an ungodly nation: O deliver me from the deceitful and unjust man. 43:2 For thou art the God of my strength: why dost thou cast me off? why go I mourning because of the oppression of the enemy? 43:3 O send out thy light and thy truth: let them lead me; let them bring me unto thy holy hill, and to thy tabernacles. 43:4 Then will I go unto the altar of God, unto God my exceeding joy: yea, upon the harp will I praise thee, O God my God. 43:5

hy art thou cast down, O my soul? and why art thou disquieted within me? hope in God: for I shall yet praise him, who is the health of my countenance, and my God.

44

e have heard with our ears, O God, our fathers have told us, what work thou didst in their days, in the times of old. 44:2 How thou didst drive out the heathen with thy hand, and plantedst them; how thou didst afflict the people, and cast them out. 44:3 For they got not the land in possession by their own sword, neither did their own arm save them: but thy right hand, and thine arm, and the light of thy countenance, because thou hadst a favour unto them. 44:4 Thou art my King, O God: command deliverances for Jacob. 44:5 Through thee will we push down our enemies: through thy name will we tread them under that rise up against us. 44:6 For I will not trust in my bow, neither shall my sword save me. 44:7 But thou hast saved us from our enemies, and hast put them to shame that hated us. 44:8 In God we boast all the day long, and praise thy name for ever. Selah. 44:9 But thou hast cast off, and put us to shame; and goest not forth with our armies. 44:10 Thou makest us to turn back from the enemy: and they which hate us spoil for themselves. 44:11 Thou hast given us like sheep appointed for meat; and hast scattered us among the heathen. 44:12 Thou sellest thy people for nought, and dost not increase thy wealth by their price. 44:13 Thou makest us a reproach to our neighbours, a scorn and a derision to them that are round about us. 44:14 Thou makest us a byword among the heathen, a shaking of the head among the people. 44:15 My confusion is continually before me, and the shame of my face hath covered me, 44:16 For the voice of him that reproacheth and blasphemeth; by reason of the enemy and avenger. 44:17 All this is come upon us; yet have we not forgotten thee, neither have we dealt falsely in thy covenant. 44:18 Our heart is not turned back, neither have our steps declined from thy way; 44:19 Though thou hast sore broken us in the place of dragons, and covered us with the shadow of death. 44:20 If we have forgotten the name of our God, or stretched out our hands to a strange god; 44:21 Shall not God search this out? for he knoweth the secrets of the heart. 44:22 Yea, for thy sake are we killed all the day long; we are counted as sheep for the slaughter. 44:23 Awake, why sleepest thou, O Lord? arise, cast us not off for ever. 44:24 Wherefore hidest thou thy face, and forgettest our affliction and our oppression? 44:25 For our soul is bowed down to the dust: our belly cleaveth unto the earth. 44:26 Arise for our help, and redeem us for thy mercies' sake.

45

My heart is inditing a good matter: I speak of the things which I have made touching the king: my tongue is the pen of a ready writer. 45:2 Thou art fairer than the children of men: grace is poured into thy lips: therefore God hath blessed thee for ever. 45:3 Gird thy sword upon thy thigh, O most mighty, with thy glory and thy majesty. 45:4 And in thy majesty ride prosperously because of truth and meekness and righteousness; and thy right hand shall teach thee terrible things. 45:5 Thine arrows are sharp in the heart of the king's enemies; whereby the people fall under thee. 45:6 Thy throne, O God, is for ever and ever: the sceptre of thy kingdom is a right sceptre. 45:7 Thou lovest righteousness, and hatest wickedness: therefore God, thy God, hath

anointed thee with the oil of gladness above thy
fellows. 45:8 All thy garments smell of
myrrh, and aloes, and cassia, out of the ivory palaces,
whereby they have made thee glad. 45:9 Kings'
daughters were among thy honourable women: upon
thy right hand did stand the queen in gold of Ophir.
45:10 Hearken, O daughter, and consider, and
incline thine ear; forget also thine own people, and
thy father's house; 45:11 So shall the king greatly
desire thy beauty: for he is thy Lord; and worship thou
him. 45:12 And the daughter of Tyre shall be
there with a gift; even the rich among the people shall
intreat thy favour. 45:13 The king's daughter
is all glorious within: her clothing is of wrought gold.
45:14 She shall be brought unto the king in
raiment of needlework: the virgins her companions
that follow her shall be brought unto thee. 45:15
With gladness and rejoicing shall they be brought:
they shall enter into the king's palace. 45:16
Instead of thy fathers shall be thy children, whom
thou mayest make princes in all the earth. 45:17
I will make thy name to be remembered in all
generations: therefore shall the people praise thee for
ever and ever.

God is our refuge and strength, a very present help in trouble. 46:2 Therefore will not we fear, though the earth be removed, and though the mountains be carried into the midst of the sea; 46:3 Though the waters thereof roar and be troubled, though the mountains shake with the swelling thereof. Selah. 46:4 There is a river, the streams whereof shall make glad the city of God, the holy place of the tabernacles of the most High. 46:5 God is in the midst of her; she shall not be moved: God shall help her, and that right early. 46:6 The heathen raged, the kingdoms were moved: he uttered his voice, the earth melted. 46:7 The LORD of hosts is with us; the God of Jacob is our refuge. Selah. 46:8 Come, behold the works of the LORD, what desolations he hath made in the earth. 46:9 He maketh wars to cease unto the end of the earth; he breaketh the bow, and cutteth the spear in sunder; he burneth the chariot in the fire. 46:10 Be still, and know that I am God: I will be exalted among the heathen, I will be exalted in the earth. 46:11 The LORD of hosts is with us; the God of Jacob is our refuge. Selah.

47

O clap your hands, all ye people; shout unto God with the voice of triumph. 47:2 For the **LORD** most high is terrible; he is a great King over all the earth. 47:3 He shall subdue the people under us, and the nations under our feet. 47:4 He shall choose our inheritance for us, the excellency of Jacob whom he loved. Selah. 47:5 God is gone up with a shout, the **LORD** with the sound of a trumpet. 47:6 Sing praises to God, sing praises: sing praises unto our King, sing praises. 47:7 For God is the King of all the earth: sing ye praises with understanding. 47:8 God reigneth over the heathen: God sitteth upon the throne of his holiness. 47:9 The princes of the people are gathered together, even the people of the God of Abraham: for the shields of the earth belong unto God: he is greatly exalted.

48

Great is the **LORD**, and greatly to be praised in the city of our God, in the mountain of his holiness. 48:2 Beautiful for situation, the joy of the whole earth, is mount Zion, on the sides of the north, the city of the great King. 48:3 God is known in her palaces for a refuge. 48:4 For, lo, the kings were assembled, they passed by together. 48:5 They saw it, and so they marvelled; they were troubled, and hasted away. 48:6 Fear took hold upon them there, and pain, as of a woman in travail. 48:7 Thou breakest the ships of Tarshish with an east wind. 48:8 As we have heard, so have we seen in the city of the LORD of hosts, in the city of our God: God will establish it for ever. Selah. 48:9 We have thought of thy lovingkindness, O God, in the midst of thy temple. 48:10 According to thy name, O God, so is thy praise unto the ends of the earth: thy right hand is full of righteousness. 48:11 Let mount Zion rejoice, let the daughters of Judah be glad, because of thy judgments. 48:12 Walk about Zion, and go round about her: tell the towers thereof. 48:13 Mark ye well her bulwarks, consider her palaces; that ye may tell it to the generation following. 48:14 For this God is our God for ever and ever: he will be our guide even unto death.

Hear this, all ye people; give ear, all ye inhabitants of the world: 49:2 Both low and high, rich and poor, together. 49:3 My mouth shall speak of wisdom; and the meditation of my heart shall be of understanding. 49:4 I will incline mine ear to a parable: I will open my dark saying upon the harp. 49:5 Wherefore should I fear in the days of evil, when the iniquity of my heels shall compass me about? 49:6 They that trust in their wealth, and boast themselves in the multitude of their riches; 49:7 None of them can by any means redeem his brother, nor give to God a ransom for him: 49:8 (For the redemption of their soul is precious, and it ceaseth for ever:) 49:9 That he should still live for ever, and not see corruption. 49:10 For he seeth that wise men die, likewise the fool and the brutish person perish, and leave their wealth to others. 49:11 Their inward thought is, that their houses shall continue for ever, and their dwelling places to all generations; they call their lands after their own names. 49:12 Nevertheless man being in honour abideth not: he is like the beasts that perish. 49:13 This their way is their folly: yet their posterity approve their sayings. Selah. 49:14 Like sheep they are laid in the grave; death shall feed on them; and the upright shall have dominion over them in the morning;

and their beauty shall consume in the grave from their dwelling. 49:15 But God will redeem my soul from the power of the grave: for he shall receive me. Selah. 49:16 Be not thou afraid when one is made rich, when the glory of his house is increased; 49:17 For when he dieth he shall carry nothing away: his glory shall not descend after him. 49:18 Though while he lived he blessed his soul: and men will praise thee, when thou doest well to thyself. 49:19 He shall go to the generation of his fathers; they shall never see light. 49:20 Man that is in honour, and understandeth not, is like the beasts that perish.

50

The mighty God, even the LORD, hath spoken, and called the earth from the rising of the sun unto the going down thereof. 50:2 Out of Zion, the perfection of beauty, God hath shined. 50:3 Our God shall come, and shall not keep silence: a fire shall devour before him, and it shall be very tempestuous round about him. 50:4 He shall call to the heavens from above, and to the earth, that he may judge his people. 50:5 Gather my saints together unto me; those that have made a covenant with me by sacrifice. 50:6 And the heavens shall declare his righteousness: for God is judge himself. Selah. 50:7 Hear, O my people, and I will speak; O Israel, and I will testify against thee: I am God, even thy God. 50:8 I will not reprove thee for thy sacrifices or thy burnt offerings, to have been continually before me. 50:9 I will take no bullock out of thy house, nor he goats out of thy folds. 50:10 For every beast of the forest is mine, and the cattle upon a thousand hills. 50:11 I know all the fowls of the mountains: and the wild beasts of the field are mine. 50:12 If I were hungry, I would not tell thee: for the world is mine, and the fulness thereof. 50:13 Will I eat the flesh of bulls, or drink the blood of goats? 50:14 Offer unto God thanksgiving; and pay thy vows unto the most High: 50:15 And call upon me in the day of trouble: I will deliver thee, and thou shalt glorify me. 50:16 But unto the wicked God saith, What hast thou to do to declare my statutes, or that thou shouldest take my covenant in thy mouth? 50:17 Seeing thou hatest instruction, and casteth my words behind thee. 50:18 When thou sawest a thief, then thou consentedst with him, and hast been partaker with adulterers. 50:19 Thou givest thy mouth to evil, and thy tongue frameth deceit. 50:20 Thou sittest and speakest against thy brother; thou slanderest thine own mother's son. 50:21

These things hast thou done, and I kept silence; thou thoughtest that I was altogether such an one as thyself: but I will reprove thee, and set them in order before thine eyes. 50:22 Now consider this, ye that forget God, lest I tear you in pieces, and there be none to deliver. 50:23 Whoso offereth praise glorifieth me: and to him that ordereth his conversation aright will I shew the salvation of God.

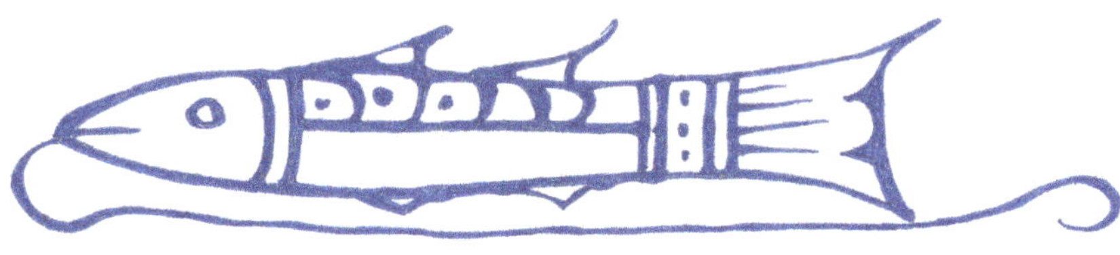

51

Have mercy upon me, O God, according to thy lovingkindness: according unto the multitude of thy tender mercies blot out my transgressions. 51:2 Wash me throughly from mine iniquity, and cleanse me from my sin. 51:3 For I acknowledge my transgressions: and my sin is ever before me. 51:4 Against thee, thee only, have I sinned, and done this evil in thy sight: that thou mightest be justified when thou speakest, and be clear when thou judgest. 51:5 Behold, I was shapen in iniquity; and in sin did my mother conceive me. 51:6 Behold, thou desirest truth in the inward parts: and in the hidden part thou shalt make me to know wisdom. 51:7 Purge me with hyssop, and I shall be clean: wash me, and I shall be whiter than snow. 51:8 Make me to hear joy and gladness; that the bones which thou hast broken may rejoice. 51:9 Hide thy face from my sins, and blot out all mine iniquities. 51:10 Create in me a clean heart, O God; and renew a right spirit within me. 51:11 Cast me not away from thy presence; and take not thy holy spirit from me. 51:12 Restore unto me the joy of thy salvation; and uphold me with thy free spirit. 51:13 Then will I teach transgressors thy ways; and sinners shall be converted unto thee. 51:14 Deliver me from bloodguiltiness, O God, thou God of my salvation: and my tongue shall sing aloud of thy righteousness. 51:15 O Lord, open thou my lips; and my mouth shall shew forth thy praise. 51:16 For thou desirest not sacrifice; else would I give it: thou delightest not in burnt offering. 51:17 The sacrifices of God are a broken spirit: a broken and a contrite heart, O God, thou wilt not despise. 51:18 Do good in thy good pleasure unto Zion: build thou the walls of Jerusalem. 51:19 Then shalt thou be pleased with the sacrifices of righteousness, with burnt offering and whole burnt offering: then shall they offer bullocks upon thine altar.

Why boastest thou thyself in mischief, O mighty man? the goodness of God endureth continually. 52:2 Thy tongue deviseth mischiefs; like a sharp razor, working deceitfully. 52:3 Thou lovest evil more than good; and lying rather than to speak righteousness. Selah. 52:4 Thou lovest all devouring words, O thou deceitful tongue. 52:5 God shall likewise destroy thee for ever, he shall take thee away, and pluck thee out of thy dwelling place, and root thee out of the land of the living. Selah. 52:6 The righteous also shall see, and fear, and shall laugh at him: 52:7 Lo, this is the man that made not God his strength; but trusted in the abundance of his riches, and strengthened himself in his wickedness. 52:8 But I am like a green olive tree in the house of God: I trust in the mercy of God for ever and ever. 52:9 I will praise thee for ever, because thou hast done it: and I will wait on thy name; for it is good before thy saints.

53

The fool hath said in his heart, There is no God. Corrupt are they, and have done abominable iniquity: there is none that doeth good. 53:2 God looked down from heaven upon the children of men, to see if there were any that did understand, that did seek God. 53:3 Every one of them is gone back: they are altogether become filthy; there is none that doeth good, no, not one. 53:4 Have the workers of iniquity no knowledge? who eat up my people as they eat bread: they have not called upon God. 53:5 There were they in great fear, where no fear was: for God hath scattered the bones of him that encampeth against thee: thou hast put them to shame, because God hath despised them. 53:6 Oh that the salvation of Israel were come out of Zion! When God bringeth back the captivity of his people, Jacob shall rejoice, and Israel shall be glad.

54

Save me, O God, by thy name, and judge me by thy strength. 54:2 Hear my prayer, O God; give ear to the words of my mouth. 54:3 For strangers are risen up against me, and oppressors seek after my soul: they have not set God before them. Selah. 54:4 Behold, God is mine helper: the Lord is with them that uphold my soul. 54:5 He shall reward evil unto mine enemies: cut them off in thy truth. 54:6 I will freely sacrifice unto thee: I will praise thy name, O LORD; for it is good. 54:7 For he hath delivered me out of all trouble: and mine eye hath seen his desire upon mine enemies.

55

Give ear to my prayer, O God; and hide not thyself from my supplication. 55:2 Attend unto me, and hear me: I mourn in my complaint, and make a noise; 55:3 Because of the voice of the enemy, because of the oppression of the wicked: for they cast iniquity upon me, and in wrath they hate me. 55:4 My heart is sore pained within me: and the terrors of death are fallen upon me. 55:5 Fearfulness and trembling are come upon me, and horror hath overwhelmed me. 55:6

And I said, Oh that I had wings like a dove! for then would I fly away, and be at rest. 55:7 Lo, then would I wander far off, and remain in the wilderness. Selah. 55:8 I would hasten my escape from the windy storm and tempest. 55:9 Destroy, O Lord, and divide their tongues: for I have seen violence and strife in the city. 55:10 Day and night they go about it upon the walls thereof: mischief also and sorrow are in the midst of it. 55:11 Wickedness is in the midst thereof: deceit and guile depart not from her streets. 55:12 For it was not an enemy that reproached me; then I could have borne it: neither was it he that hated me that did magnify himself against me; then I would have hid myself from him: 55:13 But it was thou, a man mine equal, my guide, and mine acquaintance. 55:14 We took sweet counsel together, and walked unto the house of God in company. 55:15 Let death seize upon them, and let them go down quick into hell: for wickedness is in their dwellings, and among them. 55:16 As for me, I will call upon God; and the LORD shall save me. 55:17 Evening, and morning, and at noon, will I pray, and cry aloud: and he shall hear my voice. 55:18 He hath delivered my soul in peace from the battle that was against me: for there were many with me. 55:19 God shall hear, and afflict them, even he that abideth of old. Selah. Because they have no changes, therefore they fear not God. 55:20 He hath put forth his hands against such as be at peace with him: he hath broken his covenant. 55:21 The words of his mouth were smoother than butter, but war was in his heart: his words were softer than oil, yet were they drawn swords. 55:22 Cast thy burden upon the **LORD**, and he shall sustain thee: he shall never suffer the righteous to be moved. 55:23 But thou, **O God**, shalt bring them down into the pit of destruction: bloody and deceitful men shall not live out half their days; but I will trust in thee.

56

Be merciful unto me, **O God**: for man would swallow me up; he fighting daily oppresseth me. 56:2 Mine enemies would daily swallow me up: for they be many that fight against me, **O** thou most **High**. 56:3 What time I am afraid, I will trust in thee. 56:4 In **God** I will praise his word, in **God** I have put my trust; I will not fear what flesh can do unto me. 56:5 Every day they wrest my words: all their thoughts are against me for evil. 56:6 They gather themselves together, they hide themselves, they mark my steps, when they wait for my soul. 56:7 Shall they escape by iniquity? in thine anger cast down the people, **O God.** 56:8 Thou tellest my wanderings: put thou my tears into thy bottle: are they not in thy book? 56:9 When I cry unto thee, then shall mine enemies turn back: this I know; for God is for me. 56:10 In God will I praise his word: in the **LORD** will I praise his word. 56:11 In God have I put my trust: I will not be afraid what man can do unto me. 56:12 Thy vows are upon me, **O God:** I will render praises unto thee. 56:13 For thou hast delivered my soul from death: wilt not thou deliver my feet from falling, that I may walk before God in the light of the living?

57

Be merciful unto me, **O God,** be merciful unto me: for my soul trusteth in thee: yea, in the shadow of thy wings will I make my refuge, until these calamities be overpast. 57:2 I will cry unto God most high; unto God that performeth all things for me. 57:3 He shall send from heaven, and save me from the reproach of him that would swallow me up. Selah. God shall send forth his mercy and his truth. 57:4 My soul is among lions: and I lie even among them that are set on fire, even the sons of men, whose teeth are spears and arrows, and their tongue a sharp sword. 57:5 Be thou exalted, O God, above the heavens; let thy glory be above all the earth. 57:6 They have prepared a net for my steps; my soul is bowed down: they have digged a pit before me, into the midst whereof they are fallen themselves. Selah. 57:7 My heart is fixed, O God, my heart is fixed: I will sing and give praise. 57:8 Awake up, my glory; awake, psaltery and harp: I myself will awake early. 57:9 I will praise thee, O Lord, among the people: I will sing unto thee among the nations. 57:10 For thy mercy is great unto the heavens, and thy truth unto the clouds. 57:11 Be thou exalted, O God, above the heavens: let thy glory be above all the earth.

58

Do ye indeed speak righteousness, O congregation? do ye judge uprightly, O ye sons of men? 58:2 Yea, in heart ye work wickedness; ye weigh the violence of your hands in the earth. 58:3 The wicked are estranged from the womb: they go astray as soon as they be born, speaking lies. 58:4 Their poison is like the poison of a serpent: they are like the deaf adder that stoppeth her ear; 58:5 Which will not hearken to the voice of charmers, charming never so wisely. 58:6 Break their teeth, **O God**, in their mouth: break out the great teeth of the young lions, **O LORD**. 58:7 Let them melt away as waters which run continually: when he bendeth his bow to shoot his arrows, let them be as cut in pieces. 58:8 As a snail which melteth, let every one of them pass away: like the untimely birth of a woman, that they may not see the sun. 58:9 Before your pots can feel the thorns, he shall take them away as with a whirlwind, both living, and in his wrath. 58:10 The righteous shall rejoice when he seeth the vengeance: he shall wash his feet in the blood of the wicked. 58:11 So that a man shall say, Verily there is a reward for the righteous: verily he is a God that judgeth in the earth.

Deliver me from mine enemies, O my God: defend me from them that rise up against me. 59:2 Deliver me from the workers of iniquity, and save me from bloody men. 59:3 For, lo, they lie in wait for my soul: the mighty are gathered against me; not for my transgression, nor for my sin, O LORD. 59:4 They run and prepare themselves without my fault: awake to help me, and behold. 59:5 Thou therefore, O LORD God of hosts, the God of Israel, awake to visit all the heathen: be not merciful to any wicked transgressors. Selah. 59:6 They return at evening: they make a noise like a dog, and go round about the city. 59:7 Behold, they belch out with their mouth: swords are in their lips: for who, say they, doth hear? 59:8 But thou, O LORD, shalt laugh at them; thou shalt have all the heathen in derision. 59:9 Because of his strength will I wait upon thee: for God is my defence. 59:10 The God of my mercy shall prevent me: God shall let me see my desire upon mine enemies. 59:11 Slay them not, lest my people forget: scatter them by thy power; and bring them down, O Lord our shield. 59:12 For the sin of their mouth and the words of their lips let them even be taken in their pride: and for cursing and lying which they speak. 59:13 Consume them in wrath, consume them, that they may not be: and let them know that God ruleth in Jacob unto the ends of the earth. Selah. 59:14 And at evening let them return; and let them make a noise like a dog, and go round about the city. 59:15 Let them wander up and down for meat, and grudge if they be not satisfied. 59:16 But I will sing of thy power; yea, I will sing aloud of thy mercy in the morning: for thou hast been my defence and refuge in the day of my trouble. 59:17 Unto thee, O my strength, will I sing: for God is my defence, and the God of my mercy.

60

O God, thou hast cast us off, thou hast scattered us, thou hast been displeased; O turn thyself to us again. 60:2 Thou hast made the earth to tremble; thou hast broken it: heal the breaches thereof; for it shaketh. 60:3 Thou hast shewed thy people hard things: thou hast made us to drink the wine of astonishment. 60:4 Thou hast given a banner to them that fear thee, that it may be displayed because of the truth. Selah. 60:5 That thy beloved may be delivered; save with thy right hand, and hear me. 60:6 God hath spoken in his holiness; I will rejoice, I will divide

Shechem, and mete out the valley of Succoth. 60:7 Gilead is mine, and Manasseh is mine; Ephraim also is the strength of mine head; Judah is my lawgiver; 60:8 Moab is my washpot; over Edom will I cast out my shoe: Philistia, triumph thou because of me. 60:9 Who will bring me into the strong city? who will lead me into Edom? 60:10 Wilt not thou, O God, which hadst cast us off? and thou, O God, which didst not go out with our armies? 60:11 Give us help from trouble: for vain is the help of man. 60:12 Through God we shall do valiantly: for he it is that shall tread down our enemies.

61

Hear my cry, O God; attend unto my prayer. 61:2 From the end of the earth will I cry unto thee, when my heart is overwhelmed: lead me to the rock that is higher than I. 61:3 For thou hast been a shelter for me, and a strong tower from the enemy. 61:4 I will abide in thy tabernacle for ever: I will trust in the covert of thy wings. Selah. 61:5 For thou, O God, hast heard my vows: thou hast given me the heritage of those that fear thy name. 61:6 Thou wilt prolong the king's life: and his years as many generations. 61:7 He shall abide before God for ever: O prepare mercy and truth, which may preserve him. 61:8 So will I sing praise unto thy name for ever, that I may daily perform my vows.

62

Truly my soul waiteth upon God: from him cometh my salvation. 62:2 He only is my rock and my salvation; he is my defence; I shall not be greatly moved. 62:3 How long will ye imagine mischief against a man? ye shall be slain all of you: as a bowing wall shall ye be, and as a tottering fence. 62:4 They only consult to cast him down from his excellency: they delight in lies: they bless with their mouth, but they curse inwardly. Selah. 62:5 My soul, wait thou only upon God; for my expectation is from him. 62:6 He only is my rock and my salvation: he is my defence; I shall not be moved. 62:7 In God is my salvation and my glory: the rock of my strength, and my refuge, is in God. 62:8 Trust in him at all times; ye people, pour out your heart before him: God is a refuge for us. Selah. 62:9 Surely men of low degree are vanity, and men of high degree are a lie: to be laid in the balance, they are altogether lighter than vanity. 62:10 Trust not in oppression, and become not vain in robbery: if riches increase, set not your heart upon them. 62:11 God hath spoken once; twice have I heard this; that power belongeth unto God. 62:12 Also unto thee, O Lord, belongeth mercy: for thou renderest to every man according to his work.

63

O God, thou art my God; early will I seek thee: my soul thirsteth for thee, my flesh longeth for thee in a dry and thirsty land, where no water is; 63:2 To see thy power and thy glory, so as I have seen thee in the sanctuary. 63:3 Because thy lovingkindness is better than life, my lips shall praise thee. 63:4 Thus will I bless thee while I live: I will lift up my hands in thy name. 63:5 My soul shall be satisfied as with marrow and fatness; and my mouth shall praise thee with joyful lips: 63:6

When I remember thee upon my bed, and meditate on thee in the night watches. 63:7 Because thou hast been my help, therefore in the shadow of thy wings will I rejoice. 63:8 My soul followeth hard after thee: thy right hand upholdeth me. 63:9 But those that seek my soul, to destroy it, shall go into the lower parts of the earth. 63:10 They shall fall by the sword: they shall be a portion for foxes. 63:11 But the king shall rejoice in God; every one that sweareth by him shall glory: but the mouth of them that speak lies shall be stopped.

64

Hear my voice, O God, in my prayer: preserve my life from fear of the enemy. 64:2 Hide me from the secret counsel of the wicked; from the insurrection of the workers of iniquity: 64:3 Who whet their tongue like a sword, and bend their bows to shoot their arrows, even bitter words: 64:4 That they may shoot in secret at the perfect: suddenly do they shoot at him, and fear not. 64:5 They encourage themselves in an evil matter: they commune of laying snares privily;

they say, Who shall see them? 64:6 They search out iniquities; they accomplish a diligent search: both the inward thought of every one of them, and the heart, is deep. 64:7 But God shall shoot at them with an arrow; suddenly shall they be wounded. 64:8 So they shall make their own tongue to fall upon themselves: all that see them shall flee away. 64:9 And all men shall fear, and shall declare the work of God; for they shall wisely consider of his doing. 64:10 The righteous shall be glad in the LORD, and shall trust in him; and all the upright in heart shall glory.

65

Praise waiteth for thee, O God, in Sion: and unto thee shall the vow be performed. 65:2 O thou that hearest prayer, unto thee shall all flesh come. 65:3 Iniquities prevail against me: as for our transgressions, thou shalt purge them away. 65:4 Blessed is the man whom thou choosest, and causest to approach unto thee, that he may dwell in thy courts: we shall be satisfied with the goodness of thy house, even of thy holy temple.

65:5 **B**y terrible things in righteousness wilt thou answer us, **O God** of our salvation; who art the confidence of all the ends of the earth, and of them that are afar off upon the sea: 65:6 **W**hich by his strength setteth fast the mountains; being girded with power: 65:7 **W**hich stilleth the noise of the seas, the noise of their waves, and the tumult of the people. 65:8 **T**hey also that dwell in the uttermost parts are afraid at thy tokens: thou makest the outgoings of the morning and evening to rejoice. 65:9 **T**hou visitest the earth, and waterest it: thou greatly enrichest it with the river of **God**, which is full of water: thou preparest them corn, when thou hast so provided for it. 65:10 **T**hou waterest the ridges thereof abundantly: thou settlest the furrows thereof: thou makest it soft with showers: thou blessest the springing thereof. 65:11 **T**hou crownest the year with thy goodness; and thy paths drop fatness. 65:12 **T**hey drop upon the pastures of the wilderness: and the little hills rejoice on every side. 65:13 **T**he pastures are clothed with flocks; the valleys also are covered over with corn; they shout for joy, they also sing.

Make a joyful noise unto God, all ye lands: 66:2 Sing forth the honour of his name: make his praise glorious. 66:3 Say unto God, How terrible art thou in thy works! through the greatness of thy power shall thine enemies submit themselves unto thee. 66:4 All the earth shall worship thee, and shall sing unto thee; they shall sing to thy name. Selah. 66:5 Come and see the works of God: he is terrible in his doing toward the children of men. 66:6 He turned the sea into dry land: they went through the flood on foot: there did we rejoice in him. 66:7 He ruleth by his power for ever; his eyes behold the nations: let not the rebellious exalt themselves. Selah. 66:8 O bless our God, ye people, and make the voice of his praise to be heard: 66:9 Which holdeth our soul in life, and suffereth not our feet to be moved. 66:10 For thou, O God, hast proved us: thou hast tried us, as silver is tried. 66:11 Thou broughtest us into the net; thou laidst affliction upon our loins. 66:12 Thou hast caused men to ride over our heads; we went through fire and through water: but thou broughtest us out into a wealthy place. 66:13 I will go into thy house with burnt offerings: I will pay thee my vows, 66:14 Which my lips have uttered, and my mouth hath spoken, when I was in trouble. 66:15 I will offer unto thee burnt sacrifices of fatlings, with the incense of rams; I will offer bullocks with goats. Selah. 66:16 Come and hear, all ye that fear God, and I will declare what he hath done for my soul. 66:17 I cried unto him with my mouth, and he was extolled with my tongue. 66:18 If I regard iniquity in my heart, the Lord will not hear me: 66:19 But verily God hath heard me; he hath attended to the voice of my prayer. 66:20 Blessed be God, which hath not turned away my prayer, nor his mercy from me.

67

God be merciful unto us, and bless us; and cause his face to shine upon us; Selah. 67:2 That thy way may be known upon earth, thy saving health among all nations. 67:3 Let the people praise thee, O God; let all the people praise thee. 67:4 O let the nations be glad and sing for joy: for thou shalt judge the people righteously, and govern the nations upon earth. Selah. 67:5 Let the people praise thee, O God; let all the people praise thee. 67:6 Then shall the earth yield her increase; and God, even our own God, shall bless us.

67:7 God shall bless us; and all the ends of the earth shall fear him.

68

Let God arise, let his enemies be scattered: let them also that hate him flee before him. 68:2 As smoke is driven away, so drive them away: as wax melteth before the fire, so let the wicked perish at the presence of God. 68:3 But let the righteous be glad; let them rejoice before God: yea, let them exceedingly rejoice. 68:4 Sing unto God, sing praises to his name: extol him that rideth upon the heavens by his name JAH, and rejoice before him. 68:5 A father of the fatherless, and a judge of the widows, is God in his holy habitation. 68:6 God setteth the solitary in families: he bringeth out those which are bound with chains: but the rebellious dwell in a dry land. 68:7 O God, when thou wentest forth before thy people, when thou didst march through the wilderness; Selah: 68:8 The earth shook, the heavens also dropped at the presence of God: even Sinai itself was moved at the presence of God, the God of Israel. 68:9 Thou, O God, didst send a plentiful rain, whereby thou didst confirm thine inheritance, when it was weary. 68:10 Thy congregation hath dwelt therein: thou, O God, hast prepared of thy goodness for the poor. 68:11 The Lord gave the word: great was the company of those that published it. 68:12 Kings of armies did flee apace: and she that tarried at home divided the spoil. 68:13 Though ye have lien among the pots, yet shall ye be as the wings of a dove covered with silver, and her feathers with yellow gold. 68:14 When the Almighty scattered kings in it, it was white as snow in Salmon. 68:15 The hill of God is as the hill of Bashan; an high hill as the hill of Bashan. 68:16 Why leap ye, ye high hills? this is the hill which God desireth to dwell in; yea, the LORD will dwell in it for ever. 68:17 The chariots of God are twenty thousand, even thousands of angels: the Lord is among them, as in Sinai, in the holy place. 68:18 Thou hast ascended on high, thou hast led captivity captive: thou hast received gifts for men; yea, for the rebellious also, that the LORD God might dwell among them. 68:19 Blessed be the Lord, who daily loadeth us with benefits, even the God of our salvation. Selah. 68:20 He that is our God is the God of salvation; and unto GOD the Lord belong the issues from death. 68:21 But God shall wound the head of his enemies, and the hairy scalp of such an one as goeth on still in his trespasses. 68:22 The Lord said, I will bring again from Bashan, I will bring my people again from the depths of the sea: 68:23 That thy foot may be dipped in the blood of thine enemies, and the tongue of thy dogs in the same. 68:24 They have seen thy goings, O God; even the goings of my God, my King, in the sanctuary. 68:25 The singers went before, the players on instruments followed after; among them were the damsels playing with timbrels. 68:26 Bless ye God in the congregations, even the Lord, from the fountain of Israel. 68:27 There is little Benjamin with their ruler, the princes of Judah and their council, the princes of Zebulun, and the princes of Naphtali. 68:28 Thy God hath commanded thy strength: strengthen, O God, that which thou hast wrought for us. 68:29 Because of thy temple at Jerusalem shall kings bring presents unto thee. 68:30 Rebuke the company of spearmen, the multitude of the bulls, with the calves of the people, till every one submit himself with pieces of silver: scatter thou the people that delight in war. 68:31 Princes shall come out of Egypt; Ethiopia shall soon stretch out her hands unto God. 68:32 Sing unto God, ye kingdoms of the earth; O sing praises unto the Lord; Selah: 68:33 To him that rideth upon the heavens of heavens, which were of old; lo, he doth send out his voice, and that a mighty voice. 68:34 Ascribe ye strength unto God: his excellency is over Israel, and his strength is in the clouds. 68:35 O God, thou art terrible out of thy holy places: the God of Israel is he that giveth strength and power unto his people. Blessed be God.

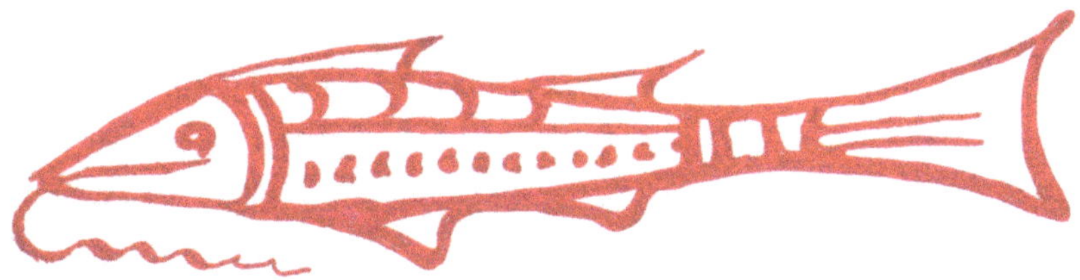

69

Save me, O God; for the waters are come in unto my soul. 69:2 I sink in deep mire, where there is no standing: I am come into deep waters, where the floods overflow me. 69:3 I am weary of my crying: my throat is dried: mine eyes fail while I wait for my God. 69:4 They that hate me without a cause are more than the hairs of mine head: they that would destroy me, being mine enemies wrongfully, are mighty: then I restored that which I took not away. 69:5 O God, thou knowest my foolishness; and my sins are not hid from thee. 69:6 Let not them that wait on thee, O Lord GOD of hosts, be ashamed for my sake: let not those that seek thee be confounded for my sake, O God of Israel. 69:7 Because for thy sake I have borne reproach; shame hath covered my face. 69:8 I am become a stranger unto my brethren, and an alien unto my mother's children. 69:9 For the zeal of thine house hath eaten me up; and the reproaches of them that reproached thee are fallen upon me. 69:10 When I wept, and chastened my soul with fasting, that was to my reproach. 69:11 I made sackcloth also my garment; and I became a proverb to them. 69:12 They that sit in the gate speak against me; and I was the song of the drunkards. 69:13 But as for me, my prayer is unto thee, O LORD, in an acceptable time: O God, in the multitude of thy mercy hear me, in the truth of thy salvation. 69:14 Deliver me out of the mire, and let me not sink: let me be delivered from them that hate me, and out of the deep waters. 69:15 Let not the waterflood overflow me, neither let the deep swallow me up, and let not the pit shut her mouth upon me. 69:16 Hear me, O LORD; for thy lovingkindness is good: turn unto me according to the multitude of thy tender mercies. 69:17 And hide not thy face from thy servant; for I am in trouble: hear me speedily. 69:18 Draw nigh unto my soul, and redeem it: deliver me because of mine enemies. 69:19 Thou hast known my reproach, and my shame, and my dishonour: mine adversaries are all before thee. 69:20 Reproach hath broken my heart; and I am full of heaviness: and I looked for some to take pity, but there was none; and for comforters, but I found none. 69:21 They gave me also gall for my meat; and in my thirst they gave me vinegar to drink. 69:22 Let their table become a snare before them: and that which should have been for their welfare, let it become a trap. 69:23 Let their eyes be darkened, that they see not; and make their loins continually to shake. 69:24 Pour out thine indignation upon them, and let thy wrathful anger take hold of them. 69:25 Let their habitation be desolate; and let none dwell in their tents. 69:26 For they persecute him whom thou hast smitten; and they talk to the grief of those whom thou hast wounded. 69:27 Add iniquity unto their iniquity: and let them not come into thy righteousness. 69:28 Let them be blotted out of the book of the living, and not be written with the righteous. 69:29 But I am poor and sorrowful: let thy salvation, O God, set me up on high. 69:30 I will praise the name of God with a song, and will magnify him with thanksgiving. 69:31 This also shall please the LORD better than an ox or bullock that hath horns and hoofs. 69:32 The humble shall see this, and be glad: and your heart shall live that seek God. 69:33 For the LORD heareth the poor, and despiseth not his prisoners. 69:34 Let the heaven and earth praise him, the seas, and every thing that moveth therein. 69:35 For God will save Zion, and will build the cities of Judah: that they may dwell there, and have it in possession. 69:36 The seed also of his servants shall inherit it: and they that love his name shall dwell therein.

70

Make haste, O God, to deliver me; make haste to help me, O LORD. 70:2 Let them be ashamed and confounded that seek after my soul: let them be turned backward, and put to confusion, that desire my hurt. 70:3 Let them be turned back for a reward of their shame that say, Aha, aha. 70:4 Let all those that seek thee rejoice and be glad in thee: and let such as love thy salvation say continually, Let God be magnified. 70:5 But I am poor and needy: make haste unto me, O God: thou art my help and my deliverer; O LORD, make no tarrying.

71

In thee, O LORD, do I put my trust: let me never be put to confusion. 71:2 Deliver me in thy righteousness, and cause me to escape: incline thine ear unto me, and save me. 71:3 Be thou my strong habitation, whereunto I may continually resort: thou hast given commandment to save me; for thou art my rock and my fortress. 71:4

Deliver me, **O my God**, out of the hand of the wicked, out of the hand of the unrighteous and cruel man. 71:5 For thou art my hope, **O Lord GOD**: thou art my trust from my youth. 71:6 By thee have I been holden up from the womb: thou art he that took me out of my mother's bowels: my praise shall be continually of thee. 71:7 I am as a wonder unto many; but thou art my strong refuge. 71:8 Let my mouth be filled with thy praise and with thy honour all the day. 71:9 Cast me not off in the time of old age; forsake me not when my strength faileth. 71:10 For mine enemies speak against me; and they that lay wait for my soul take counsel together, 71:11 Saying, **God** hath forsaken him: persecute and take him; for there is none to deliver him. 71:12 **O** God, be not far from me: **O my** God, make haste for my help. 71:13 Let them be confounded and consumed that are adversaries to my soul; let them be covered with reproach and dishonour that seek my hurt. 71:14 But I will hope continually, and will yet praise thee more and more. 71:15 My mouth shall shew forth thy righteousness and thy salvation all the day; for I know not the numbers thereof. 71:16 I will go in the strength of the Lord **GOD**: I will make mention of thy righteousness, even of thine only. 71:17 **O** God, thou hast taught me from my youth: and hitherto have I declared thy wondrous works. 71:18 Now also when I am old and greyheaded, **O**

God, forsake me not; until I have shewed thy strength unto this generation, and thy power to every one that is to come. 71:19 Thy righteousness also, O God, is very high, who hast done great things: O God, who is like unto thee! 71:20 Thou, which hast shewed me great and sore troubles, shalt quicken me again, and shalt bring me up again from the depths of the earth. 71:21 Thou shalt increase my greatness, and comfort me on every side. 71:22 I will also praise thee with the psaltery, even thy truth, O my God: unto thee will I sing with the harp, O thou Holy One of Israel. 71:23 My lips shall greatly rejoice when I sing unto thee; and my soul, which thou hast redeemed. 71:24 My tongue also shall talk of thy righteousness all the day long: for they are confounded, for they are brought unto shame, that seek my hurt.

72

Give the king thy judgments, O God, and thy righteousness unto the king's son. 72:2 He shall judge thy people with righteousness, and thy poor with judgment. 72:3

The mountains shall bring peace to the people, and the little hills, by righteousness. 72:4 He shall judge the poor of the people, he shall save the children of the needy, and shall break in pieces the oppressor. 72:5 They shall fear thee as long as the sun and moon endure, throughout all generations. 72:6 He shall come down like rain upon the mown grass: as showers that water the earth. 72:7 In his days shall the righteous flourish; and abundance of peace so long as the moon endureth. 72:8 He shall have dominion also from sea to sea, and from the river unto the ends of the earth. 72:9 They that dwell in the wilderness shall bow before him; and his enemies shall lick the dust. 72:10 The kings of Tarshish and of the isles shall bring presents: the kings of Sheba and Seba shall offer gifts. 72:11 Yea, all kings shall fall down before him: all nations shall serve him. 72:12 For he shall deliver the needy when he crieth; the poor also, and him that hath no helper. 72:13 He shall spare the poor and needy, and shall save the souls of the needy. 72:14 He shall redeem their soul from deceit and violence: and precious shall their blood be in his sight. 72:15 And he shall live, and to him shall be given of the gold of Sheba: prayer also shall be made for him continually; and daily shall he be praised. 72:16 There shall be an handful of corn in the earth upon the top of the mountains; the fruit thereof shall shake like Lebanon: and they of the city shall flourish like grass of the earth. 72:17 His name shall endure for ever: his name shall be continued as long as the sun: and men shall be blessed in him: all nations shall call him blessed. 72:18 Blessed be the **LORD** God, the God of Israel, who only doeth wondrous things. 72:19 And blessed be his glorious name for ever: and let the whole earth be filled with his glory; Amen, and Amen. 72:20 The prayers of David the son of Jesse are ended.

73

Truly God is good to Israel, even to such as are of a clean heart. 73:2 But as for me, my feet were almost gone; my steps had well nigh slipped. 73:3 For I was envious at the foolish, when I saw the prosperity of the wicked. 73:4 For there are no bands in their death: but their strength is firm. 73:5 They are not in trouble as other men; neither are they plagued like other men. 73:6 Therefore pride compasseth them about as a chain; violence covereth them as a garment. 73:7 Their eyes stand out with fatness: they have more than heart could wish. 73:8

They are corrupt, and speak wickedly concerning oppression: they speak loftily. 73:9 They set their mouth against the heavens, and their tongue walketh through the earth. 73:10 Therefore his people return hither: and waters of a full cup are wrung out to them. 73:11 And they say, How doth God know? and is there knowledge in the most High? 73:12 Behold, these are the ungodly, who prosper in the world; they increase in riches. 73:13 Verily I have cleansed my heart in vain, and washed my hands in innocency. 73:14 For all the day long have I been plagued, and chastened every morning. 73:15 If I say, I will speak thus; behold, I should offend against the generation of thy children. 73:16 When I thought to know this, it was too painful for me; 73:17 Until I went into the sanctuary of God; then understood I their end. 73:18 Surely thou didst set them in slippery places: thou castedst them down into destruction. 73:19 How are they brought into desolation, as in a moment! they are utterly consumed with terrors. 73:20 As a dream when one awaketh; so, O Lord, when thou awakest, thou shalt despise their image. 73:21 Thus my heart was grieved, and I was pricked in my reins. 73:22 So foolish was I, and ignorant: I was as a beast before thee. 73:23 Nevertheless I am continually with thee: thou hast holden me by my right hand. 73:24 Thou shalt guide me with thy counsel, and afterward receive me to glory. 73:25 Whom have I in heaven but thee? and there is none upon earth that I desire beside thee. 73:26 My flesh and my heart faileth: but God is the strength of my heart, and my portion for ever. 73:27 For, lo, they that are far from thee shall perish: thou hast destroyed all them that go a whoring from thee. 73:28 But it is good for me to draw near to God: I have put my trust in the Lord GOD, that I may declare all thy works.

74

O God, why hast thou cast us off for ever? why doth thine anger smoke against the sheep of thy pasture? 74:2 Remember thy congregation, which thou hast purchased of old; the rod of thine inheritance, which thou hast redeemed; this mount Zion, wherein thou hast dwelt. 74:3 Lift up thy feet unto the perpetual desolations; even all that the enemy hath done wickedly in the sanctuary. 74:4 Thine enemies roar in the midst of thy congregations; they set up their ensigns for signs. 74:5 A man was famous according as he had lifted up axes upon the thick trees. 74:6 But now they break down the carved work thereof at once with axes and hammers. 74:7 They have cast fire into thy sanctuary, they have defiled by casting down the dwelling place of thy name to the ground. 74:8 They said in their hearts, Let us destroy them together: they have burned up all the synagogues of God in the land. 74:9 We see not our signs: there is no more any prophet: neither is there among us any that knoweth how long. 74:10 O God, how long shall the adversary reproach? shall the enemy blaspheme thy name for ever? 74:11 Why withdrawest thou thy hand, even thy right hand? pluck it out of thy bosom. 74:12 For God is my King of old, working salvation in the midst of the earth. 74:13 Thou didst divide the sea by thy strength: thou brakest the heads of the dragons in the waters. 74:14 Thou brakest the heads of leviathan in pieces, and gavest him to be meat to the people inhabiting the wilderness. 74:15 Thou didst cleave the fountain and the flood: thou driedst up mighty rivers. 74:16 The day is thine, the night also is thine: thou hast prepared the light and the sun. 74:17 Thou hast set all the borders of the earth: thou hast made summer and winter. 74:18 Remember this, that the enemy hath reproached, O LORD, and that the foolish people have blasphemed thy name. 74:19 O deliver not the soul of thy turtledove unto the multitude of the wicked: forget not the congregation of thy poor for ever. 74:20

Have respect unto the covenant: for the dark places of the earth are full of the habitations of cruelty. 74:21 O let not the oppressed return ashamed: let the poor and needy praise thy name. 74:22 Arise, O God, plead thine own cause: remember how the foolish man reproacheth thee daily. 74:23 Forget not the voice of thine enemies: the tumult of those that rise up against thee increaseth continually.

75

Unto thee, O God, do we give thanks, unto thee do we give thanks: for that thy name is near thy wondrous works declare. 75:2 When I shall receive the congregation I will judge uprightly. 75:3 The earth and all the inhabitants thereof are dissolved: I bear up the pillars of it. Selah. 75:4 I said unto the fools, Deal not foolishly: and to the wicked, Lift not up the horn: 75:5 Lift not up your horn on high: speak not with a stiff neck. 75:6 For promotion cometh neither from the east, nor from the west, nor from the south. 75:7 But God is the judge: he putteth down one,

and setteth up another. 75:8 For in the hand
of the **LORD** there is a cup, and the wine is red; it is
full of mixture; and he poureth out of the same: but
the dregs thereof, all the wicked of the earth shall
wring them out, and drink them. 75:9 But I
will declare for ever; I will sing praises to the God of
Jacob. 75:10 All the horns of the wicked also
will I cut off; but the horns of the righteous shall be
exalted.

76

In Judah is God known: his name is great
in Israel. 76:2 In Salem also is
his tabernacle, and his dwelling place in Zion.
76:3 There brake he the arrows of the bow,
the shield, and the sword, and the battle. Selah.
76:4 Thou art more glorious and excellent than
the mountains of prey. 76:5 The stouthearted are
spoiled, they have slept their sleep: and none of the
men of might have found their hands. 76:6
At thy rebuke, O God of Jacob, both the chariot and
horse are cast into a dead sleep. 76:7 Thou, even
thou, art to be feared: and who may stand in thy

sight when once thou art angry? 76:8 Thou didst cause judgment to be heard from heaven; the earth feared, and was still. 76:9 When God arose to judgment, to save all the meek of the earth. Selah. 76:10 Surely the wrath of man shall praise thee: the remainder of wrath shalt thou restrain. 76:11 Vow, and pay unto the LORD your God: let all that be round about him bring presents unto him that ought to be feared. 76:12 He shall cut off the spirit of princes: he is terrible to the kings of the earth.

77

I cried unto God with my voice, even unto God with my voice; and he gave ear unto me. 77:2 In the day of my trouble I sought the Lord: my sore ran in the night, and ceased not: my soul refused to be comforted. 77:3 I remembered God, and was troubled: I complained, and my spirit was overwhelmed. Selah. 77:4 Thou holdest mine eyes waking: I am so troubled that I cannot speak. 77:5 I have considered the days of old, the years of ancient times. 77:6 I call to remembrance my song in the night: I commune with mine own heart: and my spirit made diligent search. 77:7 Will the Lord cast off for ever? and will he be favourable no more? 77:8 Is his mercy clean gone for ever? doth his promise fail for evermore? 77:9 Hath God forgotten to be gracious? hath he in anger shut up his tender mercies? Selah. 77:10 And I said, This is my infirmity: but I will remember the years of the right hand of the most High. 77:11 I will remember the works of the LORD: surely I will remember thy wonders of old. 77:12 I will meditate also of all thy work, and talk of thy doings. 77:13 Thy way, O God, is in the sanctuary: who is so great a God as our God? 77:14 Thou art the God that doest wonders: thou hast declared thy strength among the people. 77:15 Thou hast with thine arm redeemed thy people, the sons of Jacob and Joseph. Selah. 77:16 The waters saw thee, O God, the waters saw thee; they were afraid: the depths also were troubled. 77:17 The clouds poured out water: the skies sent out a sound: thine arrows also went abroad. 77:18 The voice of thy thunder was in the heaven: the lightnings lightened the world: the earth trembled and shook. 77:19 Thy way is in the sea, and thy path in the great waters, and thy footsteps are not known. 77:20 Thou leddest thy people like a flock by the hand of Moses and Aaron.

78

Give ear, O my people, to my law: incline your ears to the words of my mouth. 78:2 I will open my mouth in a parable: I will utter dark sayings of old: 78:3 Which we have heard and known, and our fathers have told us. 78:4 We will not hide them from their children, shewing to the generation to come the praises of the LORD, and his strength, and his wonderful works that he hath done. 78:5 For he established a testimony in Jacob, and appointed a law in Israel, which he commanded our fathers, that they should make them known to their children: 78:6 That the generation to come might know them, even the children which should be born; who should arise and declare them to their children: 78:7 That they might set their hope in God, and not forget the works of God, but keep his commandments: 78:8 And might not be as their fathers, a stubborn and rebellious generation; a generation that set not their heart aright, and whose spirit was not stedfast with God. 78:9 The children of Ephraim, being armed, and carrying bows, turned back in the day of battle.

78:10 They kept not the covenant of God, and refused to walk in his law; 78:11 And forgat his works, and his wonders that he had shewed them. 78:12 Marvellous things did he in the sight of their fathers, in the land of Egypt, in the field of Zoan. 78:13 He divided the sea, and caused them to pass through; and he made the waters to stand as an heap. 78:14 In the daytime also he led them with a cloud, and all the night with a light of fire. 78:15 He clave the rocks in the wilderness, and gave them drink as out of the great depths. 78:16 He brought streams also out of the rock, and caused waters to run down like rivers. 78:17 And they sinned yet more against him by provoking the most High in the wilderness. 78:18 And they tempted God in their heart by asking meat for their lust. 78:19 Yea, they spake against God; they said, Can God furnish a table in the wilderness? 78:20 Behold, he smote the rock, that the waters gushed out, and the streams overflowed; can he give bread also? can he provide flesh for his people? 78:21 Therefore the LORD heard this, and was wroth: so a fire was kindled against Jacob, and anger also came up against Israel; 78:22 Because they believed not in God, and trusted not in his salvation: 78:23 Though he had commanded the clouds from above, and opened the doors of heaven, 78:24 And had rained down manna upon them to eat, and had given them of the corn of heaven.

78:25 Man did eat angels' food: he sent them meat to the full. 78:26 He caused an east wind to blow in the heaven: and by his power he brought in the south wind. 78:27 He rained flesh also upon them as dust, and feathered fowls like as the sand of the sea: 78:28 And he let it fall in the midst of their camp, round about their habitations. 78:29 So they did eat, and were well filled: for he gave them their own desire; 78:30 They were not estranged from their lust. But while their meat was yet in their mouths, 78:31 The wrath of God came upon them, and slew the fattest of them, and smote down the chosen men of Israel. 78:32 For all this they sinned still, and believed not for his wondrous works. 78:33 Therefore their days did he consume in vanity, and their years in trouble. 78:34 When he slew them, then they sought him: and they returned and enquired early after God. 78:35 And they remembered that God was their rock, and the high God their redeemer. 78:36 Nevertheless they did flatter him with their mouth, and they lied unto him with their tongues. 78:37 For their heart was not right with him, neither were they stedfast in his covenant. 78:38 But he, being full of compassion, forgave their iniquity, and destroyed them not: yea, many a time turned he his anger away, and did not stir up all his wrath. 78:39 For he remembered that they were but flesh; a wind that passeth away, and cometh not again. 78:40

How oft did they provoke him in the wilderness, and grieve him in the desert! 78:41 Yea, they turned back and tempted God, and limited the Holy One of Israel. 78:42 They remembered not his hand, nor the day when he delivered them from the enemy. 78:43 How he had wrought his signs in Egypt, and his wonders in the field of Zoan: 78:44 And had turned their rivers into blood; and their floods, that they could not drink. 78:45 He sent divers sorts of flies among them, which devoured them; and frogs, which destroyed them. 78:46 He gave also their increase unto the caterpiller, and their labour unto the locust. 78:47 He destroyed their vines with hail, and their sycomore trees with frost. 78:48 He gave up their cattle also to the hail, and their flocks to hot thunderbolts. 78:49 He cast upon them the fierceness of his anger, wrath, and indignation, and trouble, by sending evil angels among them. 78:50 He made a way to his anger; he spared not their soul from death, but gave their life over to the pestilence; 78:51 And smote all the firstborn in Egypt; the chief of their strength in the tabernacles of Ham: 78:52 But made his own people to go forth like sheep, and guided them in the wilderness like a flock. 78:53 And he led them on safely, so that they feared not: but the sea overwhelmed their enemies. 78:54 And he brought them to the border of his sanctuary, even to this mountain, which his right hand had purchased.

78:55 He cast out the heathen also before them, and divided them an inheritance by line, and made the tribes of Israel to dwell in their tents. 78:56 Yet they tempted and provoked the most high God, and kept not his testimonies: 78:57 But turned back, and dealt unfaithfully like their fathers: they were turned aside like a deceitful bow. 78:58 For they provoked him to anger with their high places, and moved him to jealousy with their graven images. 78:59 When God heard this, he was wroth, and greatly abhorred Israel: 78:60 So that he forsook the tabernacle of Shiloh, the tent which he placed among men; 78:61 And delivered his strength into captivity, and his glory into the enemy's hand. 78:62 He gave his people over also unto the sword; and was wroth with his inheritance. 78:63 The fire consumed their young men; and their maidens were not given to marriage. 78:64 Their priests fell by the sword; and their widows made no lamentation. 78:65 Then the LORD awaked as one out of sleep, and like a mighty man that shouteth by reason of wine. 78:66 And he smote his enemies in the hinder parts: he put them to a perpetual reproach. 78:67 Moreover he refused the tabernacle of Joseph, and chose not the tribe of Ephraim: 78:68 But chose the tribe of Judah, the mount Zion which he loved. 78:69 And he built his sanctuary like high palaces, like the earth which he hath established for ever. 78:70 He chose David also his servant, and took him from the sheepfolds: 78:71 From following the ewes great with young he brought him to feed Jacob his people, and Israel his inheritance. 78:72 So he fed them according to the integrity of his heart; and guided them by the skilfulness of his hands.

79

O God, the heathen are come into thine inheritance; thy holy temple have they defiled; they have laid Jerusalem on heaps. 79:2 The dead bodies of thy servants have they given to be meat unto the fowls of the heaven, the flesh of thy saints unto the beasts of the earth. 79:3 Their blood have they shed like water round about Jerusalem; and there was none to bury them. 79:4 We are become a reproach to our neighbours, a scorn and derision to them that are round about us. 79:5 How long, LORD? wilt thou be angry for ever? shall thy jealousy burn like fire? 79:6 Pour out thy wrath upon the heathen that have not known thee, and upon the kingdoms that have not called upon thy name. 79:7 For they have devoured Jacob, and laid waste his dwelling place. 79:8 O remember not against us former iniquities: let thy tender mercies speedily prevent us: for we are brought very low. 79:9 Help us, O God of our salvation, for the glory of thy name: and deliver us, and purge away our sins, for thy name's sake. 79:10 Wherefore should the heathen say, Where is their God? let him be known among the heathen in our sight by the revenging of the blood of thy servants which is shed. 79:11 Let the sighing of the prisoner come before thee; according to the greatness of thy power preserve thou those that are appointed to die; 79:12 And render unto our neighbours sevenfold into their bosom their reproach, wherewith they have reproached thee, O Lord. 79:13 So we thy people and sheep of thy pasture will give thee thanks for ever: we will shew forth thy praise to all generations.

80

Give ear, O Shepherd of Israel, thou that leadest Joseph like a flock; thou that dwellest between the cherubims, shine forth. 80:2 Before Ephraim and Benjamin and

Manasseh stir up thy strength, and come and save us. 80:3 Turn us again, O God, and cause thy face to shine; and we shall be saved. 80:4 O LORD God of hosts, how long wilt thou be angry against the prayer of thy people? 80:5 Thou feedest them with the bread of tears; and givest them tears to drink in great measure. 80:6 Thou makest us a strife unto our neighbours: and our enemies laugh among themselves. 80:7 Turn us again, O God of hosts, and cause thy face to shine; and we shall be saved. 80:8 Thou hast brought a vine out of Egypt: thou hast cast out the heathen, and planted it. 80:9 Thou preparedst room before it, and didst cause it to take deep root, and it filled the land. 80:10 The hills were covered with the shadow of it, and the boughs thereof were like the goodly cedars. 80:11 She sent out her boughs unto the sea, and her branches unto the river. 80:12 Why hast thou then broken down her hedges, so that all they which pass by the way do pluck her? 80:13 The boar out of the wood doth waste it, and the wild beast of the field doth devour it. 80:14 Return, we beseech thee, O God of hosts: look down from heaven, and behold, and visit this vine; 80:15 And the vineyard which thy right hand hath planted, and the branch that thou madest strong for thyself. 80:16 It is burned with fire, it is cut down: they perish at the rebuke of thy countenance. 80:17 Let thy hand be upon the man of thy right hand, upon the son of man whom thou madest strong for thyself.  80:18 So will not we go back from thee: quicken us, and we will call upon thy name. 80:19 Turn us again, **O LORD** God of hosts, cause thy face to shine; and we shall be saved.

81

Sing aloud unto God our strength: make a joyful noise unto the God of Jacob. 81:2 Take a psalm, and bring hither the timbrel, the pleasant harp with the psaltery. 81:3 Blow up the trumpet in the new moon, in the time appointed, on our solemn feast day. 81:4 For this was a statute for Israel, and a law of the God of Jacob. 81:5 This he ordained in Joseph for a testimony, when he went out through the land of Egypt: where I heard a language that I understood not. 81:6 I removed his shoulder from the burden: his hands were delivered from the pots. 81:7 Thou calledst in trouble, and I delivered thee; I answered thee in the secret place of thunder: I proved thee at the waters of Meribah. Selah. 81:8 Hear, O my people, and I will testify unto thee: O Israel, if thou wilt hearken unto me; 81:9 There shall no strange god be in thee; neither shalt thou worship any strange god. 81:10 I am the **LORD** thy God, which brought thee out of the land of Egypt: open thy mouth wide, and I will fill it. 81:11 But my people would not hearken to my voice; and Israel would none of me. 81:12 So I gave them up unto their own hearts' lust: and they walked in their own counsels. 81:13 Oh that my people had hearkened unto me, and Israel had walked in my ways! 81:14 I should soon have subdued their enemies, and turned my hand against their adversaries. 81:15 The haters of the **LORD** should have submitted themselves unto him: but their time should have endured for ever. 81:16 He should have fed them also with the finest of the wheat: and with honey out of the rock should I have satisfied thee.

82

God standeth in the congregation of the mighty; he judgeth among the gods. 82:2 How long will ye judge unjustly, and accept the persons of the wicked? Selah. 82:3 Defend the poor and fatherless: do justice to the afflicted and needy. 82:4 Deliver the poor and needy: rid them out of the hand of the wicked. 82:5 They know not, neither will they understand; they walk on in darkness: all the foundations of the earth are out of course. 82:6 I have said, Ye are gods; and all of you are children of the most High. 82:7 But ye shall die like men, and fall like one of the princes. 82:8 Arise, O God, judge the earth: for thou shalt inherit all nations.

83

Keep not thou silence, O God: hold not thy peace, and be not still, O God. 83:2 For, lo, thine enemies make a tumult: and they that hate thee have lifted up the head. 83:3 They have taken crafty counsel against thy people, and consulted against thy hidden ones. 83:4 They have said, Come, and let us cut them off from being a nation; that the name of Israel may be no more in remembrance. 83:5 For they have consulted together with one consent: they are confederate against thee: 83:6 The tabernacles of Edom, and the Ishmaelites; of Moab, and the Hagarenes; 83:7 Gebal, and Ammon, and Amalek; the Philistines with the inhabitants of Tyre; 83:8 Assur also is joined with them: they have holpen the children of Lot. Selah. 83:9 Do unto them as unto the Midianites; as to Sisera, as to Jabin, at the brook of Kison: 83:10 Which perished at Endor: they became as dung for the earth. 83:11 Make their nobles like Oreb, and like Zeeb: yea, all their princes as Zebah, and as Zalmunna: 83:12 Who said, Let us take to ourselves the houses of God in possession. 83:13 O my God, make them like a wheel; as the stubble before the wind. 83:14 As the fire burneth a wood, and as the flame setteth the mountains on fire; 83:15 So persecute them with thy tempest, and make them afraid with thy storm. 83:16 Fill their faces with shame; that they may seek thy name, O LORD. 83:17 Let them be confounded and troubled for ever; yea, let them be put to shame, and perish: 83:18 That men may know that thou, whose name alone is JEHOVAH, art the most high over all the earth.

How amiable are thy tabernacles, **O LORD** of hosts! 84:2 My soul longeth, yea, even fainteth for the courts of the **LORD**: my heart and my flesh crieth out for the living God. 84:3 Yea, the sparrow hath found an house, and the swallow a nest for herself, where she may lay her young, even thine altars, **O LORD** of hosts, my King, and my God. 84:4 Blessed are they that dwell in thy house: they will be still praising thee. Selah. 84:5 Blessed is the man whose strength is in thee; in whose heart are the ways of them. 84:6 Who passing through the valley of Baca make it a well; the rain also filleth the pools. 84:7 They go from strength to strength, every one of them in Zion appeareth before God. 84:8 O **LORD** God of hosts, hear my prayer: give ear, **O** God of Jacob. Selah. 84:9 Behold, **O** God our shield, and look upon the face of thine anointed. 84:10 For a day in thy courts is better than a thousand. I had rather be a doorkeeper in the house of my God, than to dwell in the tents of wickedness. 84:11 For the **LORD** God is a sun and shield: the **LORD** will give grace and glory: no good thing will he withhold from them that walk uprightly. 84:12 O **LORD** of hosts, blessed is the man that trusteth in thee.

Lord, thou hast been favourable unto thy land: thou hast brought back the captivity of Jacob. 85:2 Thou hast forgiven the iniquity of thy people, thou hast covered all their sin. Selah. 85:3 Thou hast taken away all thy wrath: thou hast turned thyself from the fierceness of thine anger. 85:4 Turn us, O God of our salvation, and cause thine anger toward us to cease. 85:5 Wilt thou be angry with us for ever? wilt thou draw out thine anger to all generations? 85:6 Wilt thou not revive us again: that thy people may rejoice in thee? 85:7 Shew us thy mercy, O LORD, and grant us thy salvation. 85:8 I will hear what God the LORD will speak: for he will speak peace unto his people, and to his saints: but let them not turn again to folly. 85:9 Surely his salvation is nigh them that fear him; that glory may dwell in our land. 85:10 Mercy and truth are met together; righteousness and peace have kissed each other. 85:11 Truth shall spring out of the earth; and righteousness shall look down from heaven. 85:12 Yea, the LORD shall give that which is good; and our land shall yield her increase. 85:13 Righteousness shall go before him; and shall set us in the way of his steps.

ow down thine ear, **O LORD**, hear me: for I am poor and needy. 86:2 Preserve my soul; for I am holy: **O** thou my **God**, save thy servant that trusteth in thee. 86:3 Be merciful unto me, **O Lord**: for I cry unto thee daily. 86:4 Rejoice the soul of thy servant: for unto thee, **O Lord**, do I lift up my soul. 86:5 For thou, **Lord**, art good, and ready to forgive; and plenteous in mercy unto all them that call upon thee. 86:6 Give ear, **O LORD**, unto my prayer; and attend to the voice of my supplications. 86:7 In the day of my trouble I will call upon thee: for thou wilt answer me. 86:8 Among the gods there is none like unto thee, **O Lord**; neither are there any works like unto thy works. 86:9 All nations whom thou hast made shall come and worship before thee, **O Lord**; and shall glorify thy name. 86:10 For thou art great, and doest wondrous things: thou art **God** alone. 86:11 Teach me thy way, **O LORD**; I will walk in thy truth: unite my heart to fear thy name. 86:12 I will praise thee, **O Lord** my **God**, with all my heart: and I will glorify thy name for evermore. 86:13 For great is thy mercy toward me: and thou hast delivered my soul from the lowest hell. 86:14 **O** God, the proud are risen against me, and the assemblies of violent men have sought after my soul; and have not set thee before them. 86:15 But thou, **O Lord**, art a

God full of compassion, and gracious, long suffering, and plenteous in mercy and truth. 86:16 O turn unto me, and have mercy upon me; give thy strength unto thy servant, and save the son of thine handmaid. 86:17 Shew me a token for good; that they which hate me may see it, and be ashamed: because thou, **LORD**, hast holpen me, and comforted me.

87

His foundation is in the holy mountains. 87:2 The **LORD** loveth the gates of Zion more than all the dwellings of Jacob. 87:3 Glorious things are spoken of thee, **O** city of God. Selah. 87:4 I will make mention of Rahab and Babylon to them that know me: behold Philistia, and Tyre, with Ethiopia; this man was born there. 87:5 And of Zion it shall be said, This and that man was born in her: and the highest himself shall establish her. 87:6 The **LORD** shall count, when he writeth up the people, that this man was born there. Selah. 87:7 As well the singers as the players on instruments shall be there: all my springs are in thee.

88

O LORD God of my salvation, I have cried day and night before thee: 88:2 Let my prayer come before thee: incline thine ear unto my cry; 88:3 For my soul is full of troubles: and my life draweth nigh unto the grave. 88:4 I am counted with them that go down into the pit: I am as a man that hath no strength: 88:5 Free among the dead, like the slain that lie in the grave, whom thou rememberest no more: and they are cut off from thy hand. 88:6 Thou hast laid me in the lowest pit, in darkness, in the deeps. 88:7 Thy wrath lieth hard upon me, and thou hast afflicted me with all thy waves. Selah. 88:8 Thou hast put away mine acquaintance far from me; thou hast made me an abomination unto them: I am shut up, and I cannot come forth. 88:9 Mine eye mourneth by reason of affliction: LORD, I have called daily upon thee, I have stretched out my hands unto thee. 88:10

Wilt thou shew wonders to the dead? shall the dead arise and praise thee? Selah. 88:11 Shall thy lovingkindness be declared in the grave? or thy faithfulness in destruction? 88:12 Shall thy wonders be known in the dark? and thy righteousness in the land of forgetfulness? 88:13 But unto thee have I cried, O LORD; and in the morning shall my prayer prevent thee. 88:14 LORD, why castest thou off my soul? why hidest thou thy face from me? 88:15 I am afflicted and ready to die from my youth up: while I suffer thy terrors I am distracted. 88:16 Thy fierce wrath goeth over me; thy terrors have cut me off. 88:17 They came round about me daily like water; they compassed me about together. 88:18 Lover and friend hast thou put far from me, and mine acquaintance into darkness.

89

I will sing of the mercies of the LORD for ever: with my mouth will I make known thy faithfulness to all generations. 89:2 For I have said, Mercy shall be built up for ever: thy faithfulness shalt thou establish in the very heavens. 89:3 I have made a covenant with my chosen, I have sworn unto David my servant, 89:4 Thy seed will I establish for ever, and build up thy throne to all generations. Selah. 89:5 And the heavens shall praise thy wonders, O LORD: thy faithfulness also in the congregation of the saints. 89:6 For who in the heaven can be compared unto the LORD? who among the sons of the mighty can be likened unto the LORD? 89:7 God is greatly to be feared in the assembly of the saints, and to be had in reverence of all them that are about him. 89:8 O LORD God of hosts, who is a strong LORD like unto thee? or to thy faithfulness round about thee? 89:9 Thou rulest the raging of the sea: when the waves thereof arise, thou stillest them. 89:10 Thou hast broken Rahab in pieces, as one that is slain; thou hast scattered thine enemies with thy strong arm. 89:11 The heavens are thine, the earth also is thine: as for the world and the fulness thereof, thou hast founded them. 89:12 The north and the south thou hast created them: Tabor and Hermon shall rejoice in thy name. 89:13 Thou hast a mighty arm: strong is thy hand, and high is thy right hand. 89:14 Justice and judgment are the habitation of thy throne: mercy and truth shall go before thy face. 89:15 Blessed is the people that know the joyful sound: they shall walk, O LORD, in the light of thy countenance. 89:16 In thy name shall they rejoice all the day: and in thy righteousness shall they be exalted. 89:17 For thou art the glory of their strength: and in thy favour our horn shall be exalted. 89:18 For the LORD is our defence;

and the Holy One of Israel is our king. 89:19 Then thou spakest in vision to thy holy one, and saidst, I have laid help upon one that is mighty; I have exalted one chosen out of the people. 89:20 I have found David my servant; with my holy oil have I anointed him: 89:21 With whom my hand shall be established: mine arm also shall strengthen him. 89:22 The enemy shall not exact upon him; nor the son of wickedness afflict him. 89:23 And I will beat down his foes before his face, and plague them that hate him. 89:24 But my faithfulness and my mercy shall be with him: and in my name shall his horn be exalted. 89:25 I will set his hand also in the sea, and his right hand in the rivers. 89:26 He shall cry unto me, Thou art my father, my God, and the rock of my salvation. 89:27 Also I will make him my firstborn, higher than the kings of the earth. 89:28 My mercy will I keep for him for evermore, and my covenant shall stand fast with him. 89:29 His seed also will I make to endure for ever, and his throne as the days of heaven. 89:30 If his children forsake my law, and walk not in my judgments; 89:31 If they break my statutes, and keep not my commandments; 89:32 Then will I visit their transgression with the rod, and their iniquity with stripes. 89:33 Nevertheless my lovingkindness will I not utterly take from him, nor suffer my faithfulness to fail. 89:34 My covenant will I not break, nor alter the thing that is gone out of my lips. 89:35 Once have I sworn by my holiness that I will not lie unto David. 89:36 His seed shall endure for ever, and his throne as the sun before me. 89:37 It shall be established for ever as the moon, and as a faithful witness in heaven. Selah. 89:38 But thou hast cast off and abhorred, thou hast been wroth with thine anointed. 89:39 Thou hast made void the covenant of thy servant: thou hast profaned his crown by casting it to the ground. 89:40 Thou hast broken down all his hedges; thou hast brought his strong holds to ruin. 89:41 All that pass by the way spoil him: he is a reproach to his neighbours. 89:42 Thou hast set up the right hand of his adversaries; thou hast made all his enemies to rejoice. 89:43 Thou hast also turned the edge of his sword, and hast not made him to stand in the battle. 89:44 Thou hast made his glory to cease, and cast his throne down to the ground. 89:45 The days of his youth hast thou shortened: thou hast covered him with shame. Selah. 89:46 How long, LORD? wilt thou hide thyself for ever? shall thy wrath burn like fire? 89:47 Remember how short my time is: wherefore hast thou made all men in vain? 89:48 What man is he that liveth, and shall not see death? shall he deliver his soul from the hand of the grave? Selah. 89:49 Lord, where are thy former lovingkindnesses, which thou swarest unto David in thy truth? 89:50

Remember, Lord, the reproach of thy servants; how I do bear in my bosom the reproach of all the mighty people; 89:51 Wherewith thine enemies have reproached, O LORD; wherewith they have reproached the footsteps of thine anointed. 89:52 Blessed be the LORD for evermore. Amen, and Amen.

90

Lord, thou hast been our dwelling place in all generations. 90:2 Before the mountains were brought forth, or ever thou hadst formed the earth and the world, even from everlasting to everlasting, thou art God. 90:3 Thou turnest man to destruction; and sayest, Return, ye children of men. 90:4 For a thousand years in thy sight are but as yesterday when it is past, and as a watch in the night. 90:5 Thou carriest them away as with a flood; they are as a sleep: in the morning they are like grass which groweth up. 90:6 In the morning it flourisheth, and groweth up; in the evening it is cut down, and withereth. 90:7 For we are consumed by thine anger, and by thy wrath are we troubled. 90:8 Thou hast set our iniquities before thee, our secret sins in the light of thy countenance. 90:9 For all our days are passed away in thy wrath: we spend our years as a tale that is told. 90:10 The days of our years are threescore years and ten; and if by reason of strength they be fourscore years, yet is their strength labour and sorrow; for it is soon cut off, and we fly away. 90:11 Who knoweth the power of thine anger? even according to thy fear, so is thy wrath. 90:12 So teach us to number our days, that we may apply our hearts unto wisdom. 90:13 Return, O LORD, how long? and let it repent thee concerning thy servants. 90:14 O satisfy us early with thy mercy; that we may rejoice and be glad all our days. 90:15 Make us glad according to the days wherein thou hast afflicted us, and the years wherein we have seen evil. 90:16 Let thy work appear unto thy servants, and thy glory unto their children. 90:17 And let the beauty of the LORD our God be upon us: and establish thou the work of our hands upon us; yea, the work of our hands establish thou it.

He that dwelleth in the secret place of the most High shall abide under the shadow of the Almighty. 91:2 I will say of the LORD, He is my refuge and my fortress: my God; in him will I trust. 91:3 Surely he shall deliver thee from the snare of the fowler, and from the noisome pestilence. 91:4 He shall cover thee with his feathers, and under his wings shalt thou trust: his truth shall be thy shield and buckler. 91:5 Thou shalt not be afraid for the terror by night; nor for the arrow that flieth by day; 91:6 Nor for the pestilence that walketh in darkness; nor for the destruction that wasteth at noonday. 91:7 A thousand shall fall at thy side, and ten thousand at thy right hand; but it shall not come nigh thee. 91:8 Only with thine eyes shalt thou behold and see the reward of the wicked. 91:9 Because thou hast made the LORD, which is my refuge, even the most High, thy habitation; 91:10 There shall no evil befall thee, neither shall any plague come nigh thy dwelling. 91:11 For he shall give his angels charge over thee, to keep thee in all thy ways. 91:12 They shall bear thee up in their hands, lest thou dash thy foot against a stone. 91:13 Thou shalt tread upon the lion and adder: the young lion and the dragon shalt thou trample under feet. 91:14 Because he hath set his love upon me, therefore will I deliver him: I will set him

on high, because he hath known my name. 91:15
He shall call upon me, and I will answer him: I will be
with him in trouble; I will deliver him, and honour him.
91:16 **W**ith long life will I satisfy him, and
shew him my salvation.

92

It is a good thing to give thanks unto the
LORD, and to sing praises unto thy name, **O**
most **High**: 92:2 **T**o shew forth thy lovingkindness
in the morning, and thy faithfulness every night,
92:3 **U**pon an instrument of ten strings,
and upon the psaltery; upon the harp with a solemn
sound. 92:4 **F**or thou, **LORD**, hast made me glad
through thy work: I will triumph in the works of thy
hands. 92:5 **O** **LORD**, how great are thy
works! and thy thoughts are very deep. 92:6
A brutish man knoweth not; neither doth a fool
understand this. 92:7 **W**hen the wicked
spring as the grass, and when all the workers of
iniquity do flourish; it is that they shall be destroyed
for ever: 92:8 **B**ut thou, **LORD**, art most high
for evermore. 92:9 **F**or, lo, thine enemies, **O LORD**,

for, lo, thine enemies shall perish; all the workers of iniquity shall be scattered. 92:10 But my horn shalt thou exalt like the horn of an unicorn: I shall be anointed with fresh oil. 92:11 Mine eye also shall see my desire on mine enemies, and mine ears shall hear my desire of the wicked that rise up against me. 92:12 The righteous shall flourish like the palm tree: he shall grow like a cedar in Lebanon. 92:13 Those that be planted in the house of the **LORD** shall flourish in the courts of our God. 92:14 They shall still bring forth fruit in old age; they shall be fat and flourishing; 92:15 To shew that the **LORD** is upright: he is my rock, and there is no unrighteousness in him.

93

The **LORD** reigneth, he is clothed with majesty; the **LORD** is clothed with strength, wherewith he hath girded himself: the world also is stablished, that it cannot be moved. 93:2 Thy throne is established of old: thou art from everlasting. 93:3 The floods have lifted up, **O LORD**, the floods have lifted up their voice; the floods lift up their waves. 93:4 The **LORD** on high is mightier than the noise of many waters, yea, than the mighty waves of the sea. 93:5 Thy testimonies are very sure: holiness becometh thine house, **O LORD**, for ever.

94

O Lord God, to whom vengeance belongeth; O God, to whom vengeance belongeth, shew thyself. 94:2 Lift up thyself, thou judge of the earth: render a reward to the proud. 94:3 LORD, how long shall the wicked, how long shall the wicked triumph? 94:4 How long shall they utter and speak hard things? and all the workers of iniquity boast themselves? 94:5 They break in pieces thy people, **O LORD**, and afflict thine heritage. 94:6 They slay the widow and the stranger, and murder the fatherless. 94:7 Yet they say, The **LORD** shall not see, neither shall the God of Jacob regard it. 94:8 Understand, ye brutish among the people: and ye fools, when will ye be wise? 94:9 He that planted the ear, shall he not hear? he that formed the eye, shall he not see? 94:10

He that chastiseth the heathen, shall not he correct? he that teacheth man knowledge, shall not he know? 94:11 The **LORD** knoweth the thoughts of man, that they are vanity. 94:12 Blessed is the man whom thou chastenest, **O LORD**, and teachest him out of thy law; 94:13 That thou mayest give him rest from the days of adversity, until the pit be digged for the wicked. 94:14 For the **LORD** will not cast off his people, neither will he forsake his inheritance. 94:15 But judgment shall return unto righteousness: and all the upright in heart shall follow it. 94:16 Who will rise up for me against the evildoers? or who will stand up for me against the workers of iniquity? 94:17 Unless the **LORD** had been my help, my soul had almost dwelt in silence. 94:18 When I said, My foot slippeth; thy mercy, **O LORD**, held me up. 94:19 In the multitude of my thoughts within me thy comforts delight my soul. 94:20 Shall the throne of iniquity have fellowship with thee, which frameth mischief by a law? 94:21 They gather themselves together against the soul of the righteous, and condemn the innocent blood. 94:22 But the **LORD** is my defence; and my God is the rock of my refuge. 94:23 And he shall bring upon them their own iniquity, and shall cut them off in their own wickedness; yea, the **LORD** our God shall cut them off.

95

O come, let us sing unto the **LORD**: let us make a joyful noise to the rock of our salvation. 95:2 Let us come before his presence with thanksgiving, and make a joyful noise unto him with psalms. 95:3 For the **LORD** is a great God, and a great King above all gods. 95:4 In his hand are the deep places of the earth: the strength of the hills is his also. 95:5 The sea is his, and he made it: and his hands formed the dry land. 95:6 O come, let us worship and bow down: let us kneel before the **LORD** our maker. 95:7 For he is our God; and we are the people of his pasture, and the sheep of his hand. To day if ye will hear his voice, 95:8 Harden not your heart, as in the provocation, and as in the day of temptation in the wilderness: 95:9 When your fathers tempted me, proved me, and saw my work. 95:10 Forty years long was I grieved with this generation, and said, It is a people that do err in their heart, and they have not known my ways: 95:11 Unto whom I sware in my wrath that they should not enter into my rest.

O sing unto the **LORD** a new song: sing unto the **LORD**, all the earth. 96:2 Sing unto the **LORD**, bless his name; shew forth his salvation from day to day. 96:3 Declare his glory among the heathen, his wonders among all people. 96:4 For the **LORD** is great, and greatly to be praised: he is to be feared above all gods. 96:5 For all the gods of the nations are idols: but the **LORD** made the heavens. 96:6 Honour and majesty are before him: strength and beauty are in his sanctuary. 96:7 Give unto the **LORD**, O ye kindreds of the people, give unto the **LORD** glory and strength. 96:8 Give unto the **LORD** the glory due unto his name: bring an offering, and come into his courts. 96:9 O worship the **LORD** in the beauty of holiness: fear before him, all the earth. 96:10 Say among the heathen that the **LORD** reigneth: the world also shall be established that it shall not be moved: he shall judge the people righteously. 96:11 Let the heavens rejoice, and let the earth be glad; let the sea roar, and the fulness thereof. 96:12 Let the field be joyful, and all that is therein: then shall all the trees of the wood rejoice 96:13 Before the **LORD**: for he cometh, for he cometh to judge the earth: he shall judge the world with righteousness, and the people with his truth.

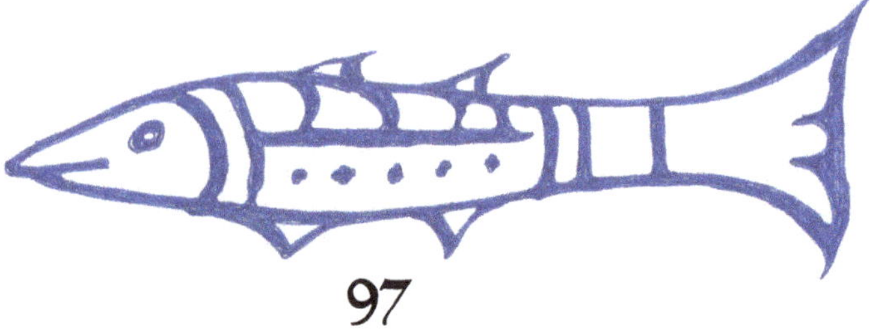

97

The **LORD** reigneth; let the earth rejoice; let the multitude of isles be glad thereof. 97:2 Clouds and darkness are round about him: righteousness and judgment are the habitation of his throne. 97:3 A fire goeth before him, and burneth up his enemies round about. 97:4 His lightnings enlightened the world: the earth saw, and trembled. 97:5 The hills melted like wax at the presence of the **LORD**, at the presence of the Lord of the whole earth. 97:6 The heavens declare his righteousness, and all the people see his glory. 97:7 Confounded be all they that serve graven images, that boast themselves of idols: worship him, all ye gods. 97:8 Zion heard, and was glad; and the daughters of Judah rejoiced because of thy judgments, **O LORD**. 97:9 For thou, **LORD**, art high above all the earth: thou art exalted far above all gods. 97:10 Ye that love the **LORD**, hate evil: he preserveth the souls of his saints; he delivereth them out of the hand of the wicked. 97:11 Light is sown for the righteous, and gladness for the upright in heart. 97:12 Rejoice in the **LORD**, ye righteous; and give thanks at the remembrance of his holiness.

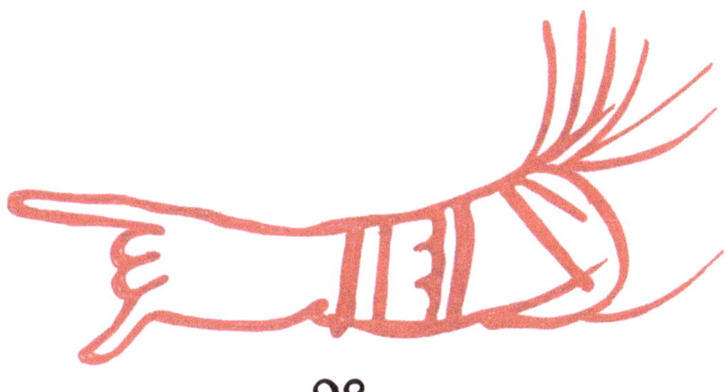

98

O sing unto the **LORD** a new song; for he hath done marvellous things: his right hand, and his holy arm, hath gotten him the victory. 98:2 The **LORD** hath made known his salvation: his righteousness hath he openly shewed in the sight of the heathen. 98:3 He hath remembered his mercy and his truth toward the house of Israel: all the ends of the earth have seen the salvation of our God. 98:4 Make a joyful noise unto the **LORD**, all the earth: make a loud noise, and rejoice, and sing praise. 98:5 Sing unto the **LORD** with the harp; with the harp, and the voice of a psalm. 98:6 With trumpets and sound of cornet make a joyful noise before the **LORD**, the King. 98:7 Let the sea roar, and the fulness thereof; the world, and they that dwell therein. 98:8 Let the floods clap their hands: let the hills be joyful together 98:9 Before the **LORD**; for he cometh to judge the earth: with righteousness shall he judge the world, and the people with equity.

99

The **LORD** reigneth; let the people tremble: he sitteth between the cherubims; let the earth be moved. 99:2 The **LORD** is great in Zion; and he is high above all the people. 99:3 Let them praise thy great and terrible name; for it is holy. 99:4 The king's strength also loveth judgment; thou dost establish equity, thou executest judgment and righteousness in Jacob. 99:5 Exalt ye the **LORD** our God, and worship at his footstool; for he is holy. 99:6 Moses and Aaron among his priests, and Samuel among them that call upon his name; they called upon the **LORD**, and he answered them. 99:7 He spake unto them in the cloudy pillar: they kept his testimonies, and the ordinance that he gave them. 99:8 Thou answeredst them, O **LORD** our God: thou wast a God that forgavest them, though thou tookest vengeance of their inventions. 99:9 Exalt the **LORD** our God, and worship at his holy hill; for the **LORD** our God is holy.

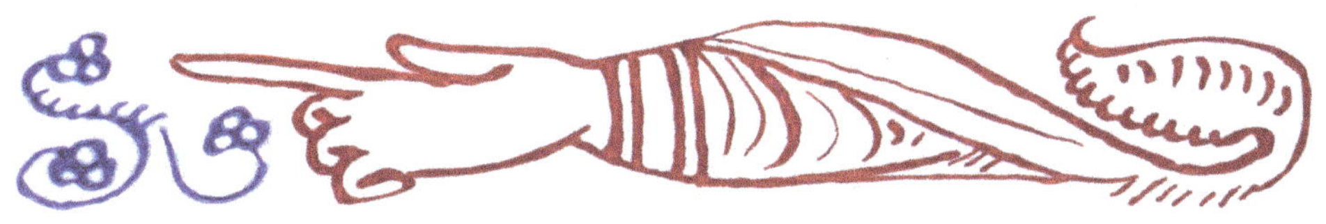

100

Make a joyful noise unto the **LORD**, all ye lands. 100:2 Serve the **LORD** with gladness: come before his presence with singing. 100:3 Know ye that the **LORD** he is God: it is he that hath made us, and not we ourselves; we are his people, and the sheep of his pasture. 100:4 Enter into his gates with thanksgiving, and into his courts with praise: be thankful unto him, and bless his name. 100:5 For the **LORD** is good; his mercy is everlasting: and his truth endureth to all generations.

101

I will sing of mercy and judgment: unto thee, **O LORD**, will I sing. 101:2 I will behave myself wisely in a perfect way. O when wilt thou come unto me? I will walk within my house with a perfect heart. 101:3 I will set no wicked thing before mine eyes: I hate the work of them that turn aside; it shall not cleave to me. 101:4 A froward heart shall depart from me: I will not know a wicked person. 101:5 Whoso privily slandereth his neighbour, him will I cut off: him that hath an high look and a proud heart will not I suffer. 101:6 Mine eyes shall be upon the faithful of the land, that they may dwell with me: he that walketh in a perfect way, he shall serve me. 101:7 He that worketh deceit shall not dwell within my house: he that telleth lies shall not tarry in my sight. 101:8 I will early destroy all the wicked of the land; that I may cut off all wicked doers from the city of the **LORD**.

102

Hear my prayer, **O LORD**, and let my cry come unto thee. 102:2 Hide not thy face from me in the day when I am in trouble; incline thine ear unto me: in the day when I call answer me speedily. 102:3 For my days are consumed like smoke, and my bones are burned as an hearth. **102:4** My heart is smitten, and withered like grass; so that I forget to eat my bread. **102:5** By reason of the voice of my groaning my bones cleave to my skin. **102:6** I am like a pelican of the wilderness: I am like an owl of the desert. **102:7** I watch, and am as a sparrow alone upon the house top. **102:8** Mine enemies reproach me all the day; and they that are mad against me are sworn against me. **102:9** For I have eaten ashes like bread, and mingled my drink with weeping, **102:10** Because of thine indignation and thy wrath: for thou hast lifted me up, and cast me down. **102:11** My days are like a shadow that declineth; and I am withered like grass. **102:12** But thou, O LORD, shalt endure for ever; and thy remembrance unto all generations. **102:13** Thou shalt arise, and have mercy upon Zion: for the time to favour her, yea, the set time, is come. **102:14** For thy servants take pleasure in her stones, and favour the dust thereof. **102:15** So the heathen shall fear the name of the LORD, and all the kings of the earth thy glory. **102:16** When the LORD shall build up Zion, he shall appear in his glory. **102:17** He will regard the prayer of the destitute, and not despise their prayer. **102:18** This shall be written for the generation to come: and the people which shall be created shall praise the LORD. **102:19** For he hath looked down from the height of his sanctuary; from heaven did

the **LORD** behold the earth; 102:20 To hear
the groaning of the prisoner; to loose those that are
appointed to death; 102:21 To declare the
name of the **LORD** in Zion, and his praise in Jerusalem;
102:22 When the people are gathered together,
and the kingdoms, to serve the **LORD**. 102:23
He weakened my strength in the way; he shortened my
days. 102:24 I said, O my God, take me not away
in the midst of my days: thy years are throughout all
generations. 102:25 Of old hast thou laid the
foundation of the earth: and the heavens are the work
of thy hands. 102:26 They shall perish, but
thou shalt endure: yea, all of them shall wax old like
a garment; as a vesture shalt thou change them, and
they shall be changed: 102:27 But thou art
the same, and thy years shall have no end. 102:28
The children of thy servants shall continue, and
their seed shall be established before thee.

103

Bless the **LORD**, **O** my soul: and all that is
within me, bless his holy name. 103:2
Bless the **LORD**, **O** my soul, and forget not all

his benefits: 103:3 Who forgiveth all thine iniquities; who healeth all thy diseases; 103:4 Who redeemeth thy life from destruction; who crowneth thee with lovingkindness and tender mercies; 103:5 Who satisfieth thy mouth with good things; so that thy youth is renewed like the eagle's. 103:6 The **LORD** executeth righteousness and judgment for all that are oppressed. 103:7 He made known his ways unto Moses, his acts unto the children of Israel. 103:8 The **LORD** is merciful and gracious, slow to anger, and plenteous in mercy. 103:9 He will not always chide: neither will he keep his anger for ever. 103:10 He hath not dealt with us after our sins; nor rewarded us according to our iniquities. 103:11 For as the heaven is high above the earth, so great is his mercy toward them that fear him. 103:12 As far as the east is from the west, so far hath he removed our transgressions from us. 103:13 Like as a father pitieth his children, so the **LORD** pitieth them that fear him. 103:14 For he knoweth our frame; he remembereth that we are dust. 103:15 As for man, his days are as grass: as a flower of the field, so he flourisheth. 103:16 For the wind passeth over it, and it is gone; and the place thereof shall know it no more. 103:17 But the mercy of the **LORD** is from everlasting to everlasting upon them that fear him, and his righteousness unto children's children; 103:18 To such as keep his covenant, and to those that remember his commandments to do them. 103:19 The **LORD** hath prepared his throne in the heavens; and his kingdom ruleth over all. 103:20 Bless the **LORD**, ye his angels, that excel in strength, that do his commandments, hearkening unto the voice of his word. 103:21 Bless ye the **LORD**, all ye his hosts; ye ministers of his, that do his pleasure. 103:22 Bless the **LORD**, all his works in all places of his dominion: bless the **LORD**, **O** my soul.

104

Bless the **LORD**, **O** my soul. **O LORD** my God, thou art very great; thou art clothed with honour and majesty. 104:2 Who coverest thyself with light as with a garment: who stretchest out the heavens like a curtain: 104:3 Who layeth the beams of his chambers in the waters: who maketh the clouds his chariot: who walketh upon the wings of the wind: 104:4 Who maketh his angels spirits; his ministers a flaming fire: 104:5 Who laid the foundations of the earth, that it should not be removed for ever. 104:6 Thou coveredst it with the deep as with a garment: the waters stood above the mountains. 104:7 At thy rebuke they fled; at the voice of thy thunder they hasted away. 104:8 They go up by the mountains; they go down by the valleys unto the place which thou hast founded for them. 104:9 Thou hast set a bound that they may not pass over; that they turn not again to cover the earth. 104:10 He sendeth the springs into the valleys, which run among the hills. 104:11 They give drink to every beast of the field: the wild asses quench their thirst. 104:12 By them shall the fowls of the heaven have their habitation, which sing among the branches. 104:13 He watereth the hills from his chambers: the earth is satisfied with the fruit of thy works. 104:14 He causeth the grass to grow for the cattle, and herb for the service of man: that he may bring forth food out of the earth; 104:15 And wine that maketh glad the heart of man, and oil to make his face to shine, and bread which strengtheneth man's heart. 104:16 The trees of the **LORD** are full of sap; the cedars of Lebanon, which he hath planted; 104:17 Where the birds make their nests: as for the stork, the fir trees are her house. 104:18 The high hills are a refuge for the wild goats; and the rocks for the conies. 104:19 He appointed the moon for seasons: the sun knoweth his going down. 104:20 Thou makest darkness, and it is night: wherein all the beasts of the forest do creep forth. 104:21 The young lions roar after their prey, and seek their meat from God. 104:22 The sun ariseth, they gather themselves together, and lay them down in their dens. 104:23 Man goeth forth unto his work and to his labour until the evening. 104:24 O LORD, how manifold are thy works! in wisdom hast thou made them all: the earth is full of thy riches. 104:25 So is this great and wide sea, wherein are things creeping innumerable, both small and great beasts. 104:26 There go the ships: there is that leviathan, whom thou hast made to play therein. 104:27 These wait all upon thee; that thou mayest give them their meat in due season. 104:28 That thou givest them they gather: thou openest thine hand, they are filled with good. 104:29 Thou hidest thy face, they are troubled: thou takest away their breath, they die, and return to their dust. 104:30 Thou sendest forth thy spirit, they are created: and thou renewest the face of the earth. 104:31 The glory of the LORD shall endure for ever: the LORD shall rejoice in his works. 104:32 He looketh on the earth, and it trembleth: he toucheth the hills, and they smoke. 104:33 I will sing unto the LORD as long as I live: I will sing praise to my God while I have my being. 104:34 My meditation of him shall be sweet: I will be glad in the LORD. 104:35 Let the sinners be consumed out of the earth, and let the wicked be no more. Bless thou the LORD, O my soul. Praise ye the LORD.

105

O give thanks unto the **LORD**; call upon his name: make known his deeds among the people. 105:2 Sing unto him, sing psalms unto him: talk ye of all his wondrous works. 105:3 Glory ye in his holy name: let the heart of them rejoice that seek the **LORD**. 105:4 Seek the **LORD**, and his strength: seek his face evermore. 105:5 Remember his marvellous works that he hath done; his wonders, and the judgments of his mouth; 105:6 O ye seed of Abraham his servant, ye children of Jacob his chosen. 105:7 He is the **LORD** our God: his judgments are in all the earth. 105:8 He hath remembered his covenant for ever, the word which he commanded to a thousand generations. 105:9 Which covenant he made with Abraham, and his oath unto Isaac; 105:10 And confirmed the same unto Jacob for a law, and to Israel for an everlasting covenant: 105:11 Saying, Unto thee will I give the land of Canaan, the lot of your inheritance: 105:12 When they were but a few men in number; yea, very few, and strangers in it. 105:13 When they went from one nation to another, from one kingdom to another people; 105:14 He suffered no man to do them wrong: yea, he reproved kings for their sakes; 105:15 Saying, Touch not mine anointed, and do my prophets no harm. 105:16 Moreover he called for a famine upon the land: he brake the whole staff of bread. 105:17 He sent a man before them, even Joseph, who was sold for a servant: 105:18 Whose feet they hurt with fetters: he was laid in iron: 105:19 Until the time that his word came: the word of the LORD tried him. 105:20 The king sent and loosed him; even the ruler of the people, and let him go free. 105:21 He made him lord of his house, and ruler of all his substance: 105:22 To bind his princes at his pleasure; and teach his senators wisdom. 105:23 Israel also came into Egypt; and Jacob sojourned in the land of Ham. 105:24 And he increased his people greatly; and made them stronger than their enemies. 105:25 He turned their heart to hate his people, to deal subtilly with his servants. 105:26 He sent Moses his servant; and Aaron whom he had chosen. 105:27 They shewed his signs among them, and wonders in the land of Ham. 105:28 He sent darkness, and made it dark; and they rebelled not against his word. 105:29 He turned their waters into blood, and slew their fish. 105:30 Their land brought forth frogs in abundance, in the chambers of their kings. 105:31 He spake, and there came divers sorts of flies, and lice in all their coasts. 105:32 He gave them hail for rain, and flaming fire in their land. 105:33 He smote their vines also and their fig trees; and brake the trees of their coasts. 105:34 He spake, and the locusts came, and caterpillers, and that without number, 105:35 And did eat up all the herbs in their land, and devoured the fruit of their ground. 105:36 He smote also all the firstborn in their land, the chief of all their strength. 105:37 He brought them forth also with silver and gold: and there was not one feeble person among their tribes. 105:38 Egypt was glad when they departed: for the fear of them fell upon them. 105:39 He spread a cloud for a covering; and fire to give light in the night. 105:40 The people asked, and he brought quails, and satisfied them with the bread of heaven. 105:41 He opened the rock, and the waters gushed out; they ran in the dry places like a river. 105:42 For he remembered his holy promise, and Abraham his servant. 105:43 And he brought forth his people with joy, and his chosen with gladness: 105:44 And gave them the lands of the heathen: and they inherited the labour of the people; 105:45 That they might observe his statutes, and keep his laws. Praise ye the **LORD**.

Praise ye the **LORD**. **O** give thanks unto the **LORD**; for he is good: for his mercy endureth for ever. 106:2 **W**ho can utter the mighty acts of the **LORD**? who can shew forth all his praise? 106:3 **B**lessed are they that keep judgment, and he that doeth righteousness at all times. 106:4 **R**emember me, **O LORD**, with the favour that thou bearest unto thy people: **O** visit me with thy salvation; 106:5 **T**hat I may see the good of thy chosen, that I may rejoice in the gladness of thy nation, that I may glory with thine inheritance. 106:6 **W**e have sinned with our fathers, we have committed iniquity, we have done wickedly. 106:7 **O**ur fathers understood not thy wonders in Egypt; they remembered not the multitude of thy mercies; but provoked him at the sea, even at the Red sea. 106:8 **N**evertheless he saved them for his name's sake, that he might make his mighty power to be known. 106:9 **H**e rebuked the Red sea also, and it was dried up: so he led them through the depths, as through the wilderness. 106:10 **A**nd he saved them from the hand of him that hated them, and redeemed them from the hand of the enemy. 106:11 **A**nd the waters covered their enemies: there was not one of them left. 106:12 **T**hen believed they his words; they sang his praise. 106:13 **T**hey soon forgat his works; they waited not for his counsel: 106:14 But lusted exceedingly in the wilderness, and tempted God in the desert. 106:15 And he gave them their request; but sent leanness into their soul. 106:16 They envied Moses also in the camp, and Aaron the saint of the **LORD**. 106:17 The earth opened and swallowed up Dathan, and covered the company of Abiram. 106:18 And a fire was kindled in their company; the flame burned up the wicked. 106:19 They made a calf in Horeb, and worshipped the molten image. 106:20 Thus they changed their glory into the similitude of an ox that eateth grass. 106:21 They forgat God their saviour, which had done great things in Egypt; 106:22 Wondrous works in the land of Ham, and terrible things by the Red sea. 106:23 Therefore he said that he would destroy them, had not Moses his chosen stood before him in the breach, to turn away his wrath, lest he should destroy them. 106:24 Yea, they despised the pleasant land, they believed not his word: 106:25 But murmured in their tents, and hearkened not unto the voice of the **LORD**. 106:26 Therefore he lifted up his hand against them, to overthrow them in the wilderness: 106:27 To overthrow their seed also among the nations, and to scatter them in the lands. 106:28 They joined themselves also unto Baalpeor, and ate the sacrifices of the dead. 106:29 Thus they provoked him to anger with their inventions: and the plague brake in upon them. 106:30 Then stood up Phinehas, and executed judgment: and so the plague was stayed. 106:31 And that was counted unto him for righteousness unto all generations for evermore. 106:32 They angered him also at the waters of strife, so that it went ill with Moses for their sakes: 106:33 Because they provoked his spirit, so that he spake unadvisedly with his lips. 106:34 They did not destroy the nations, concerning whom the LORD commanded them: 106:35 But were mingled among the heathen, and learned their works. 106:36 And they served their idols: which were a snare unto them. 106:37 Yea, they sacrificed their sons and their daughters unto devils, 106:38 And shed innocent blood, even the blood of their sons and of their daughters, whom they sacrificed unto the idols of Canaan: and the land was polluted with blood. 106:39 Thus were they defiled with their own works, and went a whoring with their own inventions. 106:40 Therefore was the wrath of the LORD kindled against his people, insomuch that he abhorred his own inheritance. 106:41 And he gave them into the hand of the heathen; and they that hated them ruled over them. 106:42 Their enemies also oppressed them, and they were brought into subjection under their hand. 106:43 Many times did he deliver them; but they provoked him with their counsel, and were brought low for their iniquity. 106:44 Nevertheless he regarded their affliction, when he heard their cry: 106:45 And he remembered for them his covenant, and repented according to the multitude of his mercies. 106:46 He made them also to be pitied of all those that carried them captives. 106:47 Save us, O LORD our God, and gather us from among the heathen, to give thanks unto thy holy name, and to triumph in thy praise. 106:48 Blessed be the LORD God of Israel from everlasting to everlasting: and let all the people say, Amen. Praise ye the LORD.

107

O give thanks unto the LORD, for he is good: for his mercy endureth for ever. 107:2 Let the redeemed of the LORD say so, whom he hath redeemed from the hand of the enemy; 107:3 And gathered them out of the lands, from the east, and from the west, from the north, and from the south. 107:4 They wandered in the wilderness in a solitary way; they found no city to dwell in. 107:5 Hungry and thirsty, their soul fainted in them. 107:6 Then they cried unto the LORD in their trouble, and he delivered them out of their distresses. 107:7 And he led them forth by the right way, that they might go to a city of habitation. 107:8 Oh that men would praise the LORD for his goodness, and for his wonderful works to the children of men! 107:9 For he satisfieth the longing soul, and filleth the hungry soul with goodness. 107:10 Such as sit in darkness and in the shadow of death, being bound in affliction and iron; 107:11 Because they rebelled against the words of God, and contemned the counsel of the most High: 107:12 Therefore he brought down their heart with labour; they fell down, and there was none to help. 107:13 Then they cried unto the LORD in their trouble, and he saved them out of their distresses. 107:14 He brought them out of darkness and the shadow of death, and brake their bands in sunder. 107:15 Oh that men would praise the LORD for his goodness, and for his wonderful works to the children of men! 107:16 For he hath broken the gates of brass, and cut the bars of iron in sunder. 107:17 Fools because of their transgression, and because of their iniquities, are afflicted. 107:18 Their soul abhorreth all manner of meat; and they draw near unto the gates of death. 107:19 Then they cry unto the LORD in their trouble, and he saveth them out of their distresses. 107:20 He sent his word, and healed them, and delivered them from their destructions. 107:21 Oh that men would praise the LORD for his goodness, and for his wonderful works to the children of men! 107:22 And let them sacrifice the sacrifices of thanksgiving, and declare his works with rejoicing. 107:23 They that go down to the sea in ships, that do business in great waters; 107:24 These see the works of the **LORD**, and his wonders in the deep. 107:25 For he commandeth, and raiseth the stormy wind, which lifteth up the waves thereof. 107:26 They mount up to the heaven, they go down again to the depths: their soul is melted because of trouble. 107:27 They reel to and fro, and stagger like a drunken man, and are at their wit's end. 107:28 Then they cry unto the **LORD** in their trouble, and he bringeth them out of their distresses. 107:29 He maketh the storm a calm, so that the waves thereof are still. 107:30 Then are they glad because they be quiet; so he bringeth them unto their desired haven. 107:31 Oh that men would praise the **LORD** for his goodness, and for his wonderful works to the children of men! 107:32 Let them exalt him also in the congregation of the people, and praise him in the assembly of the elders. 107:33 He turneth rivers into a wilderness, and the watersprings into dry ground; 107:34 A fruitful land into barrenness, for the wickedness of them that dwell therein. 107:35 He turneth the wilderness into a standing water, and dry ground into watersprings. 107:36 And there he maketh the hungry to dwell, that they may prepare a city for habitation; 107:37 And sow the fields, and plant vineyards, which may yield fruits of increase. 107:38 He blesseth them also, so that they are multiplied greatly; and suffereth not their cattle to decrease. 107:39 Again, they are minished and brought low through oppression, affliction, and sorrow. 107:40 He poureth contempt upon princes, and causeth them to wander in the wilderness, where there is no way. 107:41 Yet setteth he the poor on high from affliction, and maketh him families like a flock. 107:42 The righteous shall see it, and rejoice: and all iniquity shall stop her mouth. 107:43 Whoso is wise, and will observe these things, even they shall understand the lovingkindness of the **LORD**.

108

O God, my heart is fixed; I will sing and give praise, even with my glory. 108:2 Awake, psaltery and harp: I myself will awake early. 108:3 I will praise thee, **O LORD**, among the people: and I will sing praises unto thee among the nations. 108:4 For thy mercy is great above the heavens:

and thy truth reacheth unto the clouds. 108:5 Be thou exalted, O God, above the heavens: and thy glory above all the earth; 108:6 That thy beloved may be delivered: save with thy right hand, and answer me. 108:7 God hath spoken in his holiness; I will rejoice, I will divide Shechem, and mete out the valley of Succoth. 108:8 Gilead is mine; Manasseh is mine; Ephraim also is the strength of mine head; Judah is my lawgiver; 108:9 Moab is my washpot; over Edom will I cast out my shoe; over Philistia will I triumph. 108:10 Who will bring me into the strong city? who will lead me into Edom? 108:11 Wilt not thou, O God, who hast cast us off? and wilt not thou, O God, go forth with our hosts? 108:12 Give us help from trouble: for vain is the help of man. 108:13 Through God we shall do valiantly: for he it is that shall tread down our enemies.

109

Hold not thy peace, O God of my praise; 109:2 For the mouth of the wicked and the mouth of the deceitful are opened against me:

they have spoken against me with a lying tongue. 109:3 They compassed me about also with words of hatred; and fought against me without a cause. 109:4 For my love they are my adversaries: but I give myself unto prayer. 109:5 And they have rewarded me evil for good, and hatred for my love. 109:6 Set thou a wicked man over him: and let Satan stand at his right hand. 109:7 When he shall be judged, let him be condemned: and let his prayer become sin. 109:8 Let his days be few; and let another take his office. 109:9 Let his children be fatherless, and his wife a widow. 109:10 Let his children be continually vagabonds, and beg: let them seek their bread also out of their desolate places. 109:11 Let the extortioner catch all that he hath; and let the strangers spoil his labour. 109:12 Let there be none to extend mercy unto him: neither let there be any to favour his fatherless children. 109:13 Let his posterity be cut off; and in the generation following let their name be blotted out. 109:14 Let the iniquity of his fathers be remembered with the LORD; and let not the sin of his mother be blotted out. 109:15 Let them be before the LORD continually, that he may cut off the memory of them from the earth. 109:16 Because that he remembered not to shew mercy, but persecuted the poor and needy man, that he might even slay the broken in heart. 109:17 As he loved cursing, so let it come unto him: as he delighted not in blessing, so let it be far from him. 109:18 **A**s he clothed himself with cursing like as with his garment, so let it come into his bowels like water, and like oil into his bones. 109:19 **L**et it be unto him as the garment which covereth him, and for a girdle wherewith he is girded continually. 109:20 **L**et this be the reward of mine adversaries from the **LORD**, and of them that speak evil against my soul. 109:21 **B**ut do thou for me, **O GOD** the Lord, for thy name's sake: because thy mercy is good, deliver thou me. 109:22 **F**or I am poor and needy, and my heart is wounded within me. 109:23 **I** am gone like the shadow when it declineth: I am tossed up and down as the locust. 109:24 **M**y knees are weak through fasting; and my flesh faileth of fatness. 109:25 **I** became also a reproach unto them: when they looked upon me they shaked their heads. 109:26 **H**elp me, **O LORD** my God: **O** save me according to thy mercy: 109:27 **T**hat they may know that this is thy hand; that thou, **LORD**, hast done it. 109:28 **L**et them curse, but bless thou: when they arise, let them be ashamed; but let thy servant rejoice. 109:29 **L**et mine adversaries be clothed with shame, and let them cover themselves with their own confusion, as with a mantle. 109:30 **I** will greatly praise the **LORD** with my mouth; yea, I will praise him among the multitude. 109:31 **F**or he shall stand at the right hand of the poor, to save him from those that condemn his soul.

110

The **LORD** said unto my Lord, Sit thou at my right hand, until I make thine enemies thy footstool. 110:2 The **LORD** shall send the rod of thy strength out of Zion: rule thou in the midst of thine enemies. 110:3 Thy people shall be willing in the day of thy power, in the beauties of holiness from the womb of the morning: thou hast the dew of thy youth. 110:4 The **LORD** hath sworn, and will not repent, Thou art a priest for ever after the order of Melchizedek. 110:5 The Lord at thy right hand shall strike through kings in the day of his wrath. 110:6 He shall judge among the heathen, he shall fill the places with the dead bodies; he shall wound the heads over many countries. 110:7 He shall drink of the brook in the way: therefore shall he lift up the head.

Praise ye the **LORD**. I will praise the **LORD** with my whole heart, in the assembly of the upright, and in the congregation. 111:2 The works of the **LORD** are great, sought out of all them that have pleasure therein. 111:3 His work is honourable and glorious: and his righteousness endureth for ever. 111:4 He hath made his wonderful works to be remembered: the **LORD** is gracious and full of compassion. 111:5 He hath given meat unto them that fear him: he will ever be mindful of his covenant. 111:6 He hath shewed his people the power of his works, that he may give them the heritage of the heathen. 111:7 The works of his hands are verity and judgment; all his commandments are sure. 111:8 They stand fast for ever and ever, and are done in truth and uprightness. 111:9 He sent redemption unto his people: he hath commanded his covenant for ever: holy and reverend is his name. 111:10 The fear of the **LORD** is the beginning of wisdom: a good understanding have all they that do his commandments: his praise endureth for ever.

Praise ye the **LORD**. Blessed is the man that feareth the **LORD**, that delighteth greatly in his commandments. 112:2 His seed shall be mighty upon earth: the generation of the upright shall be blessed. 112:3 Wealth and riches shall be in his house: and his righteousness endureth for ever. 112:4 Unto the upright there ariseth light in the darkness: he is gracious, and full of compassion, and righteous. 112:5 A good man sheweth favour, and lendeth: he will guide his affairs with discretion. 112:6 Surely he shall not be moved for ever: the righteous shall be in everlasting remembrance. 112:7 He shall not be afraid of evil tidings: his heart is fixed, trusting in the **LORD**. 112:8 His heart is established, he shall not be afraid, until he see his desire upon his enemies. 112:9 He hath dispersed, he hath given to the poor; his righteousness endureth for ever; his horn shall be exalted with honour. 112:10 The wicked shall see it, and be grieved; he shall gnash with his teeth, and melt away: the desire of the wicked shall perish.

113

Praise ye the LORD. Praise, O ye servants of the LORD, praise the name of the LORD. 113:2 Blessed be the name of the LORD from this time forth and for evermore. 113:3 From the rising of the sun unto the going down of the same the LORD's name is to be praised. 113:4 The LORD is high above all nations, and his glory above the heavens. 113:5 Who is like unto the LORD our God, who dwelleth on high, 113:6 Who humbleth himself to behold the things that are in heaven, and in the earth! 113:7 He raiseth up the poor out of the dust, and lifteth the needy out of the dunghill; 113:8 That he may set him with princes, even with the princes of his people. 113:9 He maketh the barren woman to keep house, and to be a joyful mother of children. Praise ye the LORD.

114

When Israel went out of Egypt, the house of Jacob from a people of strange language; 114:2 Judah was his sanctuary, and Israel his dominion. 114:3 The sea saw it, and fled: Jordan was driven back. 114:4 The mountains skipped like rams, and the little hills like lambs. 114:5 What ailed thee, O thou sea, that thou fleddest? thou Jordan, that thou wast driven back? 114:6 Ye mountains, that ye skipped like rams; and ye little hills, like lambs? 114:7 Tremble, thou earth, at the presence of the Lord, at the presence of the God of Jacob; 114:8 Which turned the rock into a standing water, the flint into a fountain of waters.

115

Not unto us, O LORD, not unto us, but unto thy name give glory, for thy mercy, and for thy truth's sake. 115:2 Wherefore should the heathen say, Where is now their God? 115:3 But our God is in the heavens: he hath done whatsoever he hath pleased. 115:4 Their idols are silver and gold, the work of men's hands. **115:5** They have mouths, but they speak not: eyes have they, but they see not: **115:6** They have ears, but they hear not: noses have they, but they smell not: **115:7** They have hands, but they handle not: feet have they, but they walk not: neither speak they through their throat. **115:8** They that make them are like unto them; so is every one that trusteth in them. **115:9** O Israel, trust thou in the LORD: he is their help and their shield. **115:10** O house of Aaron, trust in the LORD: he is their help and their shield. **115:11** Ye that fear the LORD, trust in the LORD: he is their help and their shield. **115:12** The LORD hath been mindful of us: he will bless us; he will bless the house of Israel; he will bless the house of Aaron. **115:13** He will bless them that fear the LORD, both small and great. **115:14** The LORD shall increase you more and more, you and your children. **115:15** Ye are blessed of the LORD which made heaven and earth. **115:16** The heaven, even the heavens, are the LORD's: but the earth hath he given to the children of men. **115:17** The dead praise not the LORD, neither any that go down into silence. **115:18** But we will bless the LORD from this time forth and for evermore. Praise the LORD.

I love the **LORD**, because he hath heard my voice and my supplications. 116:2 Because he hath inclined his ear unto me, therefore will I call upon him as long as I live. 116:3 The sorrows of death compassed me, and the pains of hell gat hold upon me: I found trouble and sorrow. 116:4 Then called I upon the name of the **LORD**; **O LORD**, I beseech thee, deliver my soul. 116:5 Gracious is the **LORD**, and righteous; yea, our God is merciful. 116:6 The **LORD** preserveth the simple: I was brought low, and he helped me. 116:7 Return unto thy rest, **O** my soul; for the **LORD** hath dealt bountifully with thee. 116:8 For thou hast delivered my soul from death, mine eyes from tears, and my feet from falling. 116:9 I will walk before the **LORD** in the land of the living. 116:10 I believed, therefore have I spoken: I was greatly afflicted: 116:11 I said in my haste, All men are liars. 116:12 What shall I render unto the **LORD** for all his benefits toward me? 116:13 I will take the cup of salvation, and call upon the name of the **LORD**. 116:14 I will pay my vows unto the **LORD** now in the presence of all his people. 116:15 Precious in the sight of the **LORD** is the death of his saints. 116:16 **O LORD**, truly I am thy servant; I am thy servant, and the son of thine handmaid: thou hast loosed my bonds. 116:17 I will offer to thee the sacrifice of thanksgiving, and will call upon the name of the **LORD**. 116:18 I will pay my vows unto the **LORD** now in the presence of all his people, 116:19 In the courts of the **LORD**'s house, in the midst of thee, **O Jerusalem**. Praise ye the **LORD**.

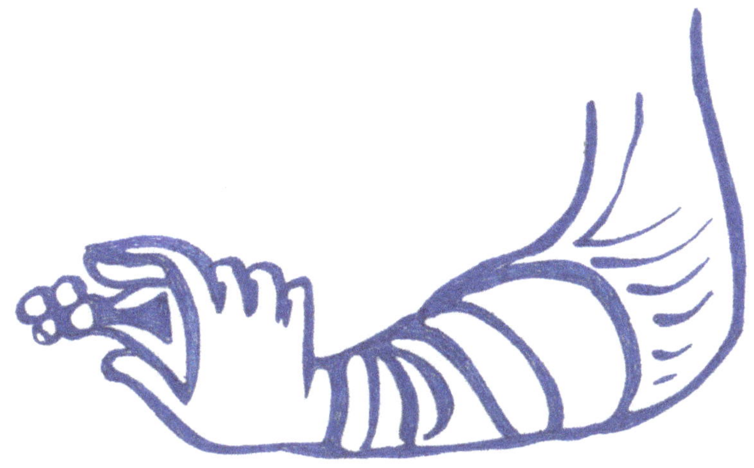

117

O Praise the **LORD**, all ye nations: praise him, all ye people. 117:2 For his merciful kindness is great toward us: and the truth of the **LORD** endureth for ever. Praise ye the **LORD**.

O give thanks unto the **LORD**; for he is good: because his mercy endureth for ever. 118:2 Let Israel now say, that his mercy endureth for ever. 118:3 Let the house of Aaron now say, that his mercy endureth for ever. 118:4 Let them now that fear the **LORD** say, that his mercy endureth for ever. 118:5 I called upon the **LORD** in distress: the **LORD** answered me, and set me in a large place. 118:6 The **LORD** is on my side; I will not fear: what can man do unto me? 118:7 The **LORD** taketh my part with them that help me: therefore shall I see my desire upon them that hate me. 118:8 It is better to trust in the **LORD** than to put confidence in man. 118:9 It is better to trust in the **LORD** than to put confidence in princes. 118:10 All nations compassed me about: but in the name of the **LORD** will I destroy them. 118:11 They compassed me about; yea, they compassed me about: but in the name of the **LORD** I will destroy them. 118:12 They compassed me about like bees; they are quenched as the fire of thorns: for in the name of the **LORD** I will destroy them. 118:13 Thou hast thrust sore at me that I might fall: but the **LORD** helped me. 118:14 The **LORD** is my strength and song, and is become my salvation. 118:15 The voice of rejoicing and salvation is in the tabernacles of the righteous: the right hand of the **LORD** doeth valiantly. 118:16 The right hand of the **LORD** is exalted: the right hand of the **LORD** doeth valiantly. 118:17 I shall not die, but live, and declare the works of the **LORD**. 118:18 The **LORD** hath chastened me sore: but he hath not given me over unto death. 118:19 Open to me the gates of righteousness: I will go into them, and I will praise the **LORD**: 118:20 This gate of the **LORD**, into which the righteous shall enter. 118:21 I will praise thee: for thou hast heard me, and art become my salvation. 118:22 The stone which the builders refused is become the head stone of the corner. 118:23 This is the **LORD**'s doing; it is marvellous in our eyes. 118:24 This is the day which the **LORD** hath made; we will rejoice and be glad in it. 118:25 Save now, I beseech thee, O **LORD**: O **LORD**, I beseech thee, send now prosperity. 118:26 Blessed be he that cometh in the name of the **LORD**: we have blessed you out of the house of the **LORD**. 118:27 God is the **LORD**, which hath shewed us light: bind the sacrifice with cords, even unto the horns of the altar. 118:28 Thou art my God, and I will praise thee: thou art my God, I will exalt thee. 118:29 O give thanks unto the **LORD**; for he is good: for his mercy endureth for ever.

119

Blessed are the undefiled in the way, who walk in the law of the **LORD**. 119:2 Blessed are they that keep his testimonies, and that seek him with the whole heart. 119:3 They also do no iniquity: they walk in his ways. 119:4 Thou hast commanded us to keep thy precepts diligently. 119:5 O that my ways were directed to keep thy statutes! 119:6 Then shall I not be ashamed, when I have respect unto all thy commandments. 119:7 I will praise thee with uprightness of heart, when I shall have learned thy righteous judgments. 119:8 I will keep thy statutes: O forsake me not utterly. 119:9 Wherewithal shall a young man cleanse his way? by taking heed thereto according to thy word. 119:10 With my whole heart have I sought thee: O let me not wander from thy commandments. 119:11 Thy word have I hid in mine heart, that I might not sin against thee. 119:12 Blessed art thou, **O LORD**: teach me thy statutes. 119:13 With my lips have I declared all the judgments of thy mouth. 119:14 I have rejoiced in the way of thy testimonies, as much as in all riches. 119:15 I will meditate in thy precepts, and have respect unto thy ways. 119:16 I will delight myself in thy statutes: I will not forget thy word. 119:17 Deal bountifully with thy servant, that I may live, and keep thy word.

119:18 Open thou mine eyes, that I may behold wondrous things out of thy law. 119:19 I am a stranger in the earth: hide not thy commandments from me. 119:20 My soul breaketh for the longing that it hath unto thy judgments at all times. 119:21 Thou hast rebuked the proud that are cursed, which do err from thy commandments. 119:22 Remove from me reproach and contempt; for I have kept thy testimonies. 119:23 Princes also did sit and speak against me: but thy servant did meditate in thy statutes. 119:24 Thy testimonies also are my delight and my counsellors. 119:25 My soul cleaveth unto the dust: quicken thou me according to thy word. 119:26 I have declared my ways, and thou heardest me: teach me thy statutes. 119:27 Make me to understand the way of thy precepts: so shall I talk of thy wondrous works. 119:28 My soul melteth for heaviness: strengthen thou me according unto thy word. 119:29 Remove from me the way of lying: and grant me thy law graciously. 119:30 I have chosen the way of truth: thy judgments have I laid before me. 119:31 I have stuck unto thy testimonies: O LORD, put me not to shame. 119:32 I will run the way of thy commandments, when thou shalt enlarge my heart. 119:33 Teach me, O LORD, the way of thy statutes; and I shall keep it unto the end. 119:34 Give me understanding, and I shall keep thy law; yea, I shall observe it with my whole heart. 119:35 Make me to go in the path of thy commandments; for therein do I delight. 119:36 Incline my heart unto thy testimonies, and not to covetousness. 119:37 Turn away mine eyes from beholding vanity; and quicken thou me in thy way. 119:38 Stablish thy word unto thy servant, who is devoted to thy fear. 119:39 Turn away my reproach which I fear: for thy judgments are good. 119:40 Behold, I have longed after thy precepts: quicken me in thy righteousness. 119:41 Let thy mercies come also unto me, O LORD, even thy salvation, according to thy word. 119:42 So shall I have wherewith to answer him that reproacheth me: for I trust in thy word. 119:43 And take not the word of truth utterly out of my mouth; for I have hoped in thy judgments. 119:44 So shall I keep thy law continually for ever and ever. 119:45 And I will walk at liberty: for I seek thy precepts. 119:46 I will speak of thy testimonies also before kings, and will not be ashamed. 119:47 And I will delight myself in thy commandments, which I have loved. 119:48 My hands also will I lift up unto thy commandments, which I have loved; and I will meditate in thy statutes. 119:49 Remember the word unto thy servant, upon which thou hast caused me to hope. 119:50 This is my comfort in my affliction: for thy word hath quickened me. 119:51 The proud have had me greatly in derision: yet have I not declined from thy law. 119:52 I remembered thy judgments of old, **O LORD**; and have comforted myself. 119:53 **H**orror hath taken hold upon me because of the wicked that forsake thy law. 119:54 **T**hy statutes have been my songs in the house of my pilgrimage. 119:55 **I** have remembered thy name, **O LORD**, in the night, and have kept thy law. 119:56 **T**his I had, because I kept thy precepts. 119:57 **T**hou art my portion, **O LORD**: I have said that I would keep thy words. 119:58 **I** intreated thy favour with my whole heart: be merciful unto me according to thy word. 119:59 **I** thought on my ways, and turned my feet unto thy testimonies. 119:60 **I** made haste, and delayed not to keep thy commandments. 119:61 **T**he bands of the wicked have robbed me: but I have not forgotten thy law. 119:62 **A**t midnight I will rise to give thanks unto thee because of thy righteous judgments. 119:63 **I** am a companion of all them that fear thee, and of them that keep thy precepts. 119:64 **T**he earth, **O LORD**, is full of thy mercy: teach me thy statutes. 119:65 **T**hou hast dealt well with thy servant, **O LORD**, according unto thy word. 119:66 **T**each me good judgment and knowledge: for I have believed thy commandments. 119:67 **B**efore I was afflicted I went astray: but now have I kept thy word. 119:68 **T**hou art good, and doest good; teach me thy statutes. 119:69 **T**he proud have forged a lie against me: but I will keep thy precepts with my whole heart. 119:70 Their heart is as fat as grease; but I delight in thy law. 119:71 It is good for me that I have been afflicted; that I might learn thy statutes. 119:72 The law of thy mouth is better unto me than thousands of gold and silver. 119:73 Thy hands have made me and fashioned me: give me understanding, that I may learn thy commandments. 119:74 They that fear thee will be glad when they see me; because I have hoped in thy word. 119:75 I know, O LORD, that thy judgments are right, and that thou in faithfulness hast afflicted me. 119:76 Let, I pray thee, thy merciful kindness be for my comfort, according to thy word unto thy servant. 119:77 Let thy tender mercies come unto me, that I may live: for thy law is my delight. 119:78 Let the proud be ashamed; for they dealt perversely with me without a cause: but I will meditate in thy precepts. 119:79 Let those that fear thee turn unto me, and those that have known thy testimonies. 119:80 Let my heart be sound in thy statutes; that I be not ashamed. 119:81 My soul fainteth for thy salvation: but I hope in thy word. 119:82 Mine eyes fail for thy word, saying, When wilt thou comfort me? 119:83 For I am become like a bottle in the smoke; yet do I not forget thy statutes. 119:84 How many are the days of thy servant? when wilt thou execute judgment on them that persecute me? 119:85 The proud have digged pits for me, which are not after thy law. 119:86 All thy commandments are faithful: they persecute me wrongfully; help thou me. 119:87 They had almost consumed me upon earth; but I forsook not thy precepts. 119:88 Quicken me after thy lovingkindness; so shall I keep the testimony of thy mouth. 119:89 For ever, O LORD, thy word is settled in heaven. 119:90 Thy faithfulness is unto all generations: thou hast established the earth, and it abideth. 119:91 They continue this day according to thine ordinances: for all are thy servants. 119:92 Unless thy law had been my delights, I should then have perished in mine affliction. 119:93 I will never forget thy precepts: for with them thou hast quickened me. 119:94 I am thine, save me; for I have sought thy precepts. 119:95 The wicked have waited for me to destroy me: but I will consider thy testimonies. 119:96 I have seen an end of all perfection: but thy commandment is exceeding broad. 119:97 O how love I thy law! it is my meditation all the day. 119:98 Thou through thy commandments hast made me wiser than mine enemies: for they are ever with me. 119:99 I have more understanding than all my teachers: for thy testimonies are my meditation. 119:100 I understand more than the ancients, because I keep thy precepts. 119:101 I have refrained my feet from every evil way, that I might keep thy word. 119:102 I have not departed from thy judgments:

for thou hast taught me. 119:103 How sweet are thy words unto my taste! yea, sweeter than honey to my mouth! 119:104 Through thy precepts I get understanding: therefore I hate every false way. 119:105 Thy word is a lamp unto my feet, and a light unto my path. 119:106 I have sworn, and I will perform it, that I will keep thy righteous judgments. 119:107 I am afflicted very much: quicken me, O LORD, according unto thy word. 119:108 Accept, I beseech thee, the freewill offerings of my mouth, O LORD, and teach me thy judgments. 119:109 My soul is continually in my hand: yet do I not forget thy law. 119:110 The wicked have laid a snare for me: yet I erred not from thy precepts. 119:111 Thy testimonies have I taken as an heritage for ever: for they are the rejoicing of my heart. 119:112 I have inclined mine heart to perform thy statutes alway, even unto the end. 119:113 I hate vain thoughts: but thy law do I love. 119:114 Thou art my hiding place and my shield: I hope in thy word. 119:115 Depart from me, ye evildoers: for I will keep the commandments of my God. 119:116 Uphold me according unto thy word, that I may live: and let me not be ashamed of my hope. 119:117 Hold thou me up, and I shall be safe: and I will have respect unto thy statutes continually. 119:118 Thou hast trodden down all them that err from thy statutes: for their deceit is falsehood. 119:119 Thou puttest away all the wicked of the earth like dross: therefore I love thy testimonies. 119:120 My flesh trembleth for fear of thee; and I am afraid of thy judgments. 119:121 I have done judgment and justice: leave me not to mine oppressors. 119:122 Be surety for thy servant for good: let not the proud oppress me. 119:123 Mine eyes fail for thy salvation, and for the word of thy righteousness. 119:124 Deal with thy servant according unto thy mercy, and teach me thy statutes. 119:125 I am thy servant; give me understanding, that I may know thy testimonies. 119:126 It is time for thee, LORD, to work: for they have made void thy law. 119:127 Therefore I love thy commandments above gold; yea, above fine gold. 119:128 Therefore I esteem all thy precepts concerning all things to be right; and I hate every false way. 119:129 Thy testimonies are wonderful: therefore doth my soul keep them. 119:130 The entrance of thy words giveth light; it giveth understanding unto the simple. 119:131 I opened my mouth, and panted: for I longed for thy commandments. 119:132 Look thou upon me, and be merciful unto me, as thou usest to do unto those that love thy name. 119:133 Order my steps in thy word: and let not any iniquity have dominion over me. 119:134 Deliver me from the oppression of man: so will I keep thy precepts. 119:135 Make thy face to shine upon thy servant; and teach me thy statutes. 119:136 Rivers of waters run down mine eyes, because they keep not thy law. 119:137 Righteous art thou, **O LORD**, and upright are thy judgments. 119:138 Thy testimonies that thou hast commanded are righteous and very faithful. 119:139 My zeal hath consumed me, because mine enemies have forgotten thy words. 119:140 Thy word is very pure: therefore thy servant loveth it. 119:141 I am small and despised: yet do not I forget thy precepts. 119:142 Thy righteousness is an everlasting righteousness, and thy law is the truth. 119:143 Trouble and anguish have taken hold on me: yet thy commandments are my delights. 119:144 The righteousness of thy testimonies is everlasting: give me understanding, and I shall live. 119:145 I cried with my whole heart; hear me, **O LORD**: I will keep thy statutes. 119:146 I cried unto thee; save me, and I shall keep thy testimonies. 119:147 I prevented the dawning of the morning, and cried: I hoped in thy word. 119:148 Mine eyes prevent the night watches, that I might meditate in thy word. 119:149 Hear my voice according unto thy lovingkindness: **O LORD**, quicken me according to thy judgment. 119:150 They draw nigh that follow after mischief: they are far from thy law. 119:151 Thou art near, **O LORD**; and all thy commandments are truth. 119:152 Concerning thy testimonies, I have known of old that thou hast founded them for ever. 119:153 Consider mine affliction, and deliver me: for I do not forget thy law. 119:154 **P**lead my cause, and deliver me: quicken me according to thy word. 119:155 **S**alvation is far from the wicked: for they seek not thy statutes. 119:156 **G**reat are thy tender mercies, **O LORD**: quicken me according to thy judgments. 119:157 **M**any are my persecutors and mine enemies; yet do I not decline from thy testimonies. 119:158 **I** beheld the transgressors, and was grieved; because they kept not thy word. 119:159 **C**onsider how I love thy precepts: quicken me, **O LORD**, according to thy lovingkindness. 119:160 **T**hy word is true from the beginning: and every one of thy righteous judgments endureth for ever. 119:161 **P**rinces have persecuted me without a cause: but my heart standeth in awe of thy word. 119:162 **I** rejoice at thy word, as one that findeth great spoil. 119:163 **I** hate and abhor lying: but thy law do I love. 119:164 **S**even times a day do I praise thee because of thy righteous judgments. 119:165 **G**reat peace have they which love thy law: and nothing shall offend them. 119:166 **L**ORD, I have hoped for thy salvation, and done thy commandments. 119:167 **M**y soul hath kept thy testimonies; and I love them exceedingly. 119:168 **I** have kept thy precepts and thy testimonies: for all my ways are before thee. 119:169 **L**et my cry come near before thee, **O LORD**: give me understanding according to thy word. 119:170 **L**et my supplication come before thee:

deliver me according to thy word. 119:171 **My** lips shall utter praise, when thou hast taught me thy statutes. 119:172 **My** tongue shall speak of thy word: for all thy commandments are righteousness. 119:173 **Let** thine hand help me; for I have chosen thy precepts. 119:174 **I** have longed for thy salvation, **O LORD**; and thy law is my delight. 119:175 **Let** my soul live, and it shall praise thee; and let thy judgments help me. 119:176 **I** have gone astray like a lost sheep; seek thy servant; for I do not forget thy commandments.

120

In my distress I cried unto the **LORD**, and he heard me. 120:2 **D**eliver my soul, **O LORD**, from lying lips, and from a deceitful tongue. 120:3 **W**hat shall be given unto thee? or what shall be done unto thee, thou false tongue? 120:4 **S**harp arrows of the mighty, with coals of juniper. 120:5 **W**oe is me, that I sojourn in **Mesech**, that I dwell in the tents of **Kedar**! 120:6 **My** soul hath long dwelt with him that hateth peace. 120:7 **I** am for peace: but when I speak, they are for war.

121

I will lift up mine eyes unto the hills, from whence cometh my help. 121:2 My help cometh from the **LORD**, which made heaven and earth. 121:3 He will not suffer thy foot to be moved: he that keepeth thee will not slumber. 121:4 Behold, he that keepeth Israel shall neither slumber nor sleep. 121:5 The **LORD** is thy keeper: the **LORD** is thy shade upon thy right hand. 121:6 The sun shall not smite thee by day, nor the moon by night. 121:7 The **LORD** shall preserve thee from all evil: he shall preserve thy soul. 121:8 The **LORD** shall preserve thy going out and thy coming in from this time forth, and even for evermore.

122

I was glad when they said unto me, Let us go into the house of the **LORD**. 122:2 Our feet shall stand within thy gates, **O** Jerusalem. 122:3 Jerusalem is builded as a city that is compact together: 122:4 Whither the tribes go up, the tribes of the **LORD**, unto the testimony of Israel, to give thanks unto the name of the **LORD**. 122:5 For there are set thrones of judgment, the thrones of the house of David. 122:6 Pray for the peace of Jerusalem: they shall prosper that love thee. 122:7 Peace be within thy walls, and prosperity within thy palaces. 122:8 For my brethren and companions' sakes, I will now say, Peace be within thee. 122:9 Because of the house of the **LORD** our God I will seek thy good.

123

Unto thee lift I up mine eyes, **O** thou that dwellest in the heavens. 123:2 Behold, as the eyes of servants look unto the hand of their masters, and as the eyes of a maiden unto the hand of her mistress; so our eyes wait upon the **LORD** our God, until that he have mercy upon us. 123:3 **H**ave mercy upon us, **O LORD**, have mercy upon us: for we are exceedingly filled with contempt. 123:4 **O**ur soul is exceedingly filled with the scorning of those that are at ease, and with the contempt of the proud.

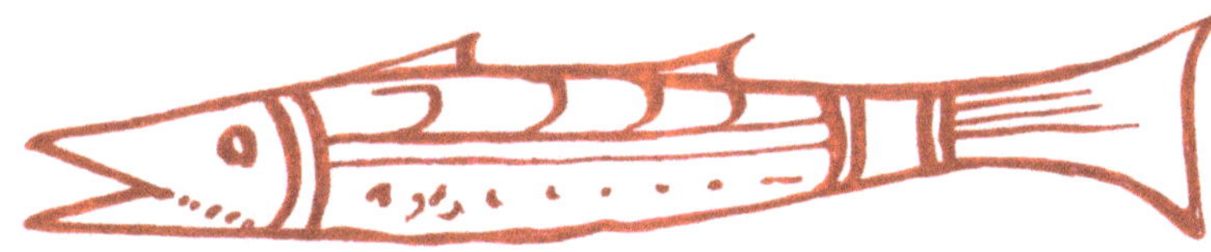

124

If it had not been the **LORD** who was on our side, now may Israel say; 124:2 **I**f it had not been the **LORD** who was on our side, when men rose up against us: 124:3 **T**hen they had swallowed us up quick, when their wrath was kindled against us: 124:4 **T**hen the waters had overwhelmed us, the stream had gone over our soul: 124:5 **T**hen the proud waters had gone over our soul. 124:6 **B**lessed be the **LORD**, who hath not given us as a prey to their teeth. 124:7 **O**ur soul is escaped as a bird out of the snare of the fowlers: the snare is broken, and we are escaped. 124:8 **O**ur help is in the name of the **LORD**, who made heaven and earth.

125

They that trust in the **LORD** shall be as mount **Z**ion, which cannot be removed, but abideth for ever. 125:2 As the mountains are round about Jerusalem, so the **LORD** is round about his people from henceforth even for ever. 125:3 For the rod of the wicked shall not rest upon the lot of the righteous; lest the righteous put forth their hands unto iniquity. 125:4 Do good, **O LORD**, unto those that be good, and to them that are upright in their hearts. 125:5 As for such as turn aside unto their crooked ways, the **LORD** shall lead them forth with the workers of iniquity: but peace shall be upon Israel.

126

When the **LORD** turned again the captivity of Zion, we were like them that dream. 126:2 Then was our mouth filled with laughter, and our tongue with singing: then said they among the heathen, The **LORD** hath done great things for them. 126:3 The **LORD** hath done great things for us; whereof we are glad. 126:4 Turn again our captivity, **O LORD**, as the streams in the south. 126:5 They that sow in tears shall reap in joy. 126:6 He that goeth forth and weepeth, bearing precious seed, shall doubtless come again with rejoicing, bringing his sheaves with him.

127

Except the **LORD** build the house, they labour in vain that build it: except the **LORD** keep the city, the watchman waketh but in vain. 127:2 It is vain for you to rise up early, to sit up late, to eat the bread of sorrows: for so he giveth his beloved sleep. 127:3 Lo, children are an heritage of the **LORD**: and the fruit of the womb is his reward. 127:4 As arrows are in the hand of a mighty man; so are children of the youth. 127:5 Happy is the man that hath his quiver full of them: they shall not be ashamed, but they shall speak with the enemies in the gate.

128

Blessed is every one that feareth the **LORD**; that walketh in his ways. 128:2 For thou shalt eat the labour of thine hands: happy shalt thou be, and it shall be well with thee. 128:3 Thy wife shall be as a fruitful vine by the sides of thine house: thy children like olive plants round about thy table. 128:4 Behold, that thus shall the man be blessed that feareth the **LORD**. 128:5 The **LORD** shall bless thee out of **Zion**: and thou shalt see the good of Jerusalem all the days of thy life. 128:6 Yea, thou shalt see thy children's children, and peace upon Israel.

129

Many a time have they afflicted me from my youth, may Israel now say: 129:2 Many a time have they afflicted me from my youth: yet they have not prevailed against me. 129:3 The plowers plowed upon my back: they made long their furrows. 129:4 The LORD is righteous: he hath cut asunder the cords of the wicked. 129:5 Let them all be confounded and turned back that hate Zion. 129:6 Let them be as the grass upon the housetops, which withereth afore it groweth up: 129:7 Wherewith the mower filleth not his hand; nor he that bindeth sheaves his bosom. 129:8 Neither do they which go by say, The blessing of the LORD be upon you: we bless you in the name of the LORD.

130

Out of the depths have I cried unto thee, O LORD. 130:2 Lord, hear my voice: let thine ears be attentive to the voice of my supplications. 130:3 If thou, LORD, shouldest mark iniquities, O Lord, who shall stand? 130:4 But there is forgiveness with thee, that thou mayest be feared. 130:5 I wait for the LORD, my soul doth wait, and in his word do I hope. 130:6 My soul waiteth for the Lord more than they that watch for the morning: I say, more than they that watch for the morning. 130:7 Let Israel hope in the LORD: for with the LORD there is mercy, and with him is plenteous redemption. 130:8 And he shall redeem Israel from all his iniquities.

131

Lord, my heart is not haughty, nor mine eyes lofty: neither do I exercise myself in great matters, or in things too high for me. 131:2 Surely I have behaved and quieted myself, as a child that is weaned of his mother: my soul is even as a weaned child. 131:3 Let Israel hope in the LORD from henceforth and for ever.

Lord, remember David, and all his afflictions: 132:2 How he sware unto the **LORD**, and vowed unto the mighty God of Jacob; 132:3 Surely I will not come into the tabernacle of my house, nor go up into my bed; 132:4 I will not give sleep to mine eyes, or slumber to mine eyelids, 132:5 Until I find out a place for the **LORD**, an habitation for the mighty God of Jacob. 132:6 Lo, we heard of it at Ephratah: we found it in the fields of the wood. 132:7 We will go into his tabernacles: we will worship at his footstool. 132:8 Arise, **O LORD**, into thy rest; thou, and the ark of thy strength. 132:9 Let thy priests be clothed with righteousness; and let thy saints shout for joy. 132:10 For thy servant David's sake turn not away the face of thine anointed. 132:11 The **LORD** hath sworn in truth unto David; he will not turn from it; Of the fruit of thy body will I set upon thy throne. 132:12 If thy children will keep my covenant and my testimony that I shall teach them, their children shall also sit upon thy throne for evermore. 132:13 For the **LORD** hath chosen Zion; he hath desired it for his habitation. 132:14 This is my rest for ever: here will I dwell; for I have desired it. 132:15 I will abundantly bless her provision: I will satisfy her poor with bread. 132:16 I will also clothe her priests with salvation: and her saints shall shout aloud for joy. 132:17 There will I make the horn of David to bud: I have ordained a lamp for mine anointed. 132:18 His enemies will I clothe with shame: but upon himself shall his crown flourish.

133

Behold, how good and how pleasant it is for brethren to dwell together in unity! 133:2 It is like the precious ointment upon the head, that ran down upon the beard, even Aaron's beard: that went down to the skirts of his garments; 133:3 As the dew of Hermon, and as the dew that descended upon the mountains of Zion: for there the LORD commanded the blessing, even life for evermore.

134

Behold, bless ye the **LORD**, all ye servants of the **LORD**, which by night stand in the house of the **LORD**. 134:2 **L**ift up your hands in the sanctuary, and bless the **LORD**. 134:3 **T**he **LORD** that made heaven and earth bless thee out of Zion.

135

Praise ye the **LORD**. Praise ye the name of the **LORD**; praise him, O ye servants of the **LORD**. 135:2 **Y**e that stand in the house of the **LORD**, in the courts of the house of our God, 135:3 **P**raise the **LORD**; for the **LORD** is good: sing praises unto his name; for it is pleasant. 135:4 **F**or the **LORD** hath chosen Jacob unto himself, and Israel for his peculiar treasure. 135:5 **F**or I know that the **LORD** is great, and that our Lord is above all gods. 135:6 **W**hatsoever the **LORD** pleased, that did he in heaven, and in earth, in the seas, and all deep places. 135:7 **H**e causeth the vapours to ascend from the ends of the earth; he maketh lightnings for the rain; he bringeth the wind out of his treasuries. 135:8 **W**ho smote the firstborn of Egypt, both of man and beast. 135:9 **W**ho sent tokens and wonders into the midst of thee, **O Egypt,** upon **Pharaoh,** and upon all his servants. 135:10 **W**ho smote great nations, and slew mighty kings; 135:11 **S**ihon king of the **Amorites,** and **Og** king of **Bashan,** and all the kingdoms of **Canaan:** 135:12 **A**nd gave their land for an heritage, an heritage unto Israel his people. 135:13 **T**hy name, **O LORD,** endureth for ever; and thy memorial, **O LORD,** throughout all generations. 135:14 **F**or the **LORD** will judge his people, and he will repent himself concerning his servants. 135:15 **T**he idols of the heathen are silver and gold, the work of men's hands. 135:16 **T**hey have mouths, but they speak not; eyes have they, but they see not; 135:17 **T**hey have ears, but they hear not; neither is there any breath in their mouths. 135:18 **T**hey that make them are like unto them: so is every one that trusteth in them. 135:19 **B**less the **LORD, O** house of Israel: bless the **LORD, O** house of **Aaron:** 135:20 **B**less the **LORD, O** house of **Levi:** ye that fear the **LORD,** bless the **LORD.** 135:21 **B**lessed be the **LORD** out of **Zion,** which dwelleth at Jerusalem. Praise ye the **LORD.**

O give thanks unto the **LORD**; for he is good: for his mercy endureth for ever. 136:2 O give thanks unto the God of gods: for his mercy endureth for ever. 136:3 O give thanks to the Lord of lords: for his mercy endureth for ever. 136:4 To him who alone doeth great wonders: for his mercy endureth for ever. 136:5 To him that by wisdom made the heavens: for his mercy endureth for ever. 136:6 To him that stretched out the earth above the waters: for his mercy endureth for ever. 136:7 To him that made great lights: for his mercy endureth for ever: 136:8 The sun to rule by day: for his mercy endureth for ever: 136:9 The moon and stars to rule by night: for his mercy endureth for ever. 136:10 To him that smote Egypt in their firstborn: for his mercy endureth for ever: 136:11 And brought out Israel from among them: for his mercy endureth for ever: 136:12 With a strong hand, and with a stretched out arm: for his mercy endureth for ever. 136:13 To him which divided the Red sea into parts: for his mercy endureth for ever: 136:14 And made Israel to pass through the midst of it: for his mercy endureth for ever: 136:15 But overthrew Pharaoh and his host in the Red sea: for his mercy endureth for ever. 136:16 To him which led his people through the wilderness: for his mercy endureth for ever. 136:17 To him which smote great kings: for his mercy endureth for ever: 136:18 And slew famous kings: for his mercy endureth for ever: 136:19 Sihon king of the Amorites: for his mercy endureth for ever: 136:20 And Og the king of Bashan: for his mercy endureth for ever: 136:21 And gave their land for an heritage: for his mercy endureth for ever: 136:22 Even an heritage unto Israel his servant: for his mercy endureth for ever. 136:23 Who remembered us in our low estate: for his mercy endureth for ever: 136:24 And hath redeemed us from our enemies: for his mercy endureth for ever. 136:25 Who giveth food to all flesh: for his mercy endureth for ever. 136:26 O give thanks unto the God of heaven: for his mercy endureth for ever.

137

By the rivers of Babylon, there we sat down, yea, we wept, when we remembered Zion. 137:2 We hanged our harps upon the willows in the midst thereof. 137:3 For there they that carried us away captive required of us a song; and they that wasted us required of us mirth, saying, Sing us one of the songs of Zion. 137:4 How shall we sing the **LORD**'s song in a strange land? 137:5 If I forget thee, O Jerusalem, let my right hand forget her cunning. 137:6 If I do not remember thee, let my tongue cleave to the roof of my mouth; if I prefer not Jerusalem above my chief joy. 137:7 Remember, **O LORD**, the children of Edom in the day of Jerusalem; who said, Rase it, rase it, even to the foundation thereof. 137:8 O daughter of Babylon, who art to be destroyed; happy shall he be, that rewardeth thee as thou hast served us. 137:9 Happy shall he be, that taketh and dasheth thy little ones against the stones.

138

I will praise thee with my whole heart: before the gods will I sing praise unto thee. 138:2 I will worship toward thy holy temple, and praise thy name for thy lovingkindness and for thy truth: for thou hast magnified thy word above all thy name. 138:3 In the day when I cried thou answeredst me, and strengthenedst me with strength in my soul. 138:4 **A**ll the kings of the earth shall praise thee, **O LORD**, when they hear the words of thy mouth. 138:5 **Y**ea, they shall sing in the ways of the **LORD**: for great is the glory of the **LORD**. 138:6 **T**hough the **LORD** be high, yet hath he respect unto the lowly: but the proud he knoweth afar off. 138:7 **T**hough I walk in the midst of trouble, thou wilt revive me: thou shalt stretch forth thine hand against the wrath of mine enemies, and thy right hand shall save me. 138:8 **T**he **LORD** will perfect that which concerneth me: thy mercy, **O LORD**, endureth for ever: forsake not the works of thine own hands.

139

O LORD, thou hast searched me, and known me. 139:2 **T**hou knowest my downsitting and mine uprising, thou understandest my thought afar off. 139:3 **T**hou compassest my path and my lying down, and art acquainted with all my ways. 139:4 **F**or there is not a word in my tongue, but, lo, **O LORD**, thou knowest it altogether. 139:5 **T**hou hast beset me behind and before, and laid thine hand upon me. 139:6 Such knowledge is too wonderful for me; it is high, I cannot attain unto it. 139:7 Whither shall I go from thy spirit? or whither shall I flee from thy presence? 139:8 If I ascend up into heaven, thou art there: if I make my bed in hell, behold, thou art there. 139:9 If I take the wings of the morning, and dwell in the uttermost parts of the sea; 139:10 Even there shall thy hand lead me, and thy right hand shall hold me. 139:11 If I say, Surely the darkness shall cover me; even the night shall be light about me. 139:12 Yea, the darkness hideth not from thee; but the night shineth as the day: the darkness and the light are both alike to thee. 139:13 For thou hast possessed my reins: thou hast covered me in my mother's womb. 139:14 I will praise thee; for I am fearfully and wonderfully made: marvellous are thy works; and that my soul knoweth right well. 139:15 My substance was not hid from thee, when I was made in secret, and curiously wrought in the lowest parts of the earth. 139:16 Thine eyes did see my substance, yet being unperfect; and in thy book all my members were written, which in continuance were fashioned, when as yet there was none of them. 139:17 How precious also are thy thoughts unto me, O God! how great is the sum of them! 139:18 If I should count them, they are more in number than the sand: when I awake, I am still with thee. 139:19 Surely thou wilt slay the wicked, O God: depart from me therefore, ye bloody men. 139:20 For they speak against thee wickedly, and thine enemies take thy name in vain. 139:21 Do not I hate them, O LORD, that hate thee? and am not I grieved with those that rise up against thee? 139:22 I hate them with perfect hatred: I count them mine enemies. 139:23 Search me, O God, and know my heart: try me, and know my thoughts: 139:24 And see if there be any wicked way in me, and lead me in the way everlasting.

140

Deliver me, O LORD, from the evil man: preserve me from the violent man; 140:2 Which imagine mischiefs in their heart; continually are they gathered together for war. 140:3 They have sharpened their tongues like a serpent; adders' poison is under their lips. Selah. 140:4 Keep me, O LORD, from the hands of the wicked; preserve me from the violent man; who have purposed to overthrow my goings. 140:5 The proud have hid a snare for me, and cords; they have spread a net by the wayside; they have set gins for me. Selah. **140:6** I said unto the **LORD**, Thou art my God: hear the voice of my supplications, **O LORD**. **140:7** O **GOD** the Lord, the strength of my salvation, thou hast covered my head in the day of battle. **140:8** Grant not, **O LORD**, the desires of the wicked: further not his wicked device; lest they exalt themselves. Selah. **140:9** As for the head of those that compass me about, let the mischief of their own lips cover them. **140:10** Let burning coals fall upon them: let them be cast into the fire; into deep pits, that they rise not up again. **140:11** Let not an evil speaker be established in the earth: evil shall hunt the violent man to overthrow him. **140:12** I know that the **LORD** will maintain the cause of the afflicted, and the right of the poor. **140:13** Surely the righteous shall give thanks unto thy name: the upright shall dwell in thy presence.

141

Lord, I cry unto thee: make haste unto me; give ear unto my voice, when I cry unto thee. **141:2** Let my prayer be set forth before thee as incense; and the lifting up of my hands as the evening sacrifice. 141:3 **S**et a watch, **O LORD**, before my mouth; keep the door of my lips. 141:4 **I**ncline not my heart to any evil thing, to practise wicked works with men that work iniquity: and let me not eat of their dainties. 141:5 **L**et the righteous smite me; it shall be a kindness: and let him reprove me; it shall be an excellent oil, which shall not break my head: for yet my prayer also shall be in their calamities. 141:6 **W**hen their judges are overthrown in stony places, they shall hear my words; for they are sweet. 141:7 **O**ur bones are scattered at the grave's mouth, as when one cutteth and cleaveth wood upon the earth. 141:8 **B**ut mine eyes are unto thee, **O GOD** the Lord: in thee is my trust; leave not my soul destitute. 141:9 **K**eep me from the snares which they have laid for me, and the gins of the workers of iniquity. 141:10 **L**et the wicked fall into their own nets, whilst that I withal escape.

142

I cried unto the **LORD** with my voice; with my voice unto the **LORD** did I make my supplication. 142:2 **I** poured out my complaint before him; I shewed before him my trouble. 142:3 When my spirit was overwhelmed within me, then thou knewest my path. In the way wherein I walked have they privily laid a snare for me. 142:4 I looked on my right hand, and beheld, but there was no man that would know me: refuge failed me; no man cared for my soul. 142:5 I cried unto thee, O LORD: I said, Thou art my refuge and my portion in the land of the living. 142:6 Attend unto my cry; for I am brought very low: deliver me from my persecutors; for they are stronger than I. 142:7 Bring my soul out of prison, that I may praise thy name: the righteous shall compass me about; for thou shalt deal bountifully with me.

143

Hear my prayer, O LORD, give ear to my supplications: in thy faithfulness answer me, and in thy righteousness. 143:2 And enter not into judgment with thy servant: for in thy sight shall no man living be justified. 143:3 For the enemy hath persecuted my soul; he hath smitten my life down to the ground; he hath made me to dwell in darkness, as those that have been long dead. 143:4 **T**herefore is my spirit overwhelmed within me; my heart within me is desolate. 143:5 **I** remember the days of old; I meditate on all thy works; I muse on the work of thy hands. 143:6 **I** stretch forth my hands unto thee: my soul thirsteth after thee, as a thirsty land. Selah. 143:7 **H**ear me speedily, **O LORD**: my spirit faileth: hide not thy face from me, lest I be like unto them that go down into the pit. 143:8 **C**ause me to hear thy lovingkindness in the morning; for in thee do I trust: cause me to know the way wherein I should walk; for I lift up my soul unto thee. 143:9 **D**eliver me, **O LORD**, from mine enemies: I flee unto thee to hide me. 143:10 **T**each me to do thy will; for thou art my God: thy spirit is good; lead me into the land of uprightness. 143:11 **Q**uicken me, **O LORD**, for thy name's sake: for thy righteousness' sake bring my soul out of trouble. 143:12 **A**nd of thy mercy cut off mine enemies, and destroy all them that afflict my soul: for I am thy servant.

Blessed be the **LORD** my strength, which teacheth my hands to war, and my fingers to fight: 144:2 My goodness, and my fortress; my high tower, and my deliverer; my shield, and he in whom I trust; who subdueth my people under me. 144:3 LORD, what is man, that thou takest knowledge of him! or the son of man, that thou makest account of him! 144:4 Man is like to vanity: his days are as a shadow that passeth away. 144:5 Bow thy heavens, **O LORD**, and come down: touch the mountains, and they shall smoke. 144:6 Cast forth lightning, and scatter them: shoot out thine arrows, and destroy them. 144:7 Send thine hand from above; rid me, and deliver me out of great waters, from the hand of strange children; 144:8 Whose mouth speaketh vanity, and their right hand is a right hand of falsehood. 144:9 I will sing a new song unto thee, **O God**: upon a psaltery and an instrument of ten strings will I sing praises unto thee. 144:10 It is he that giveth salvation unto kings: who delivereth David his servant from the hurtful sword. 144:11 Rid me, and deliver me from the hand of strange children, whose mouth speaketh vanity, and their right hand is a right hand of falsehood: 144:12 That our sons may be as plants grown up in their youth; that our daughters may be as corner stones, polished after the similitude of a palace: 144:13 That our garners may be full, affording all manner of store: that our sheep may bring forth thousands and ten thousands in our streets: 144:14 That our oxen may be strong to labour; that there be no breaking in, nor going out; that there be no complaining in our streets. 144:15 Happy is that people, that is in such a case: yea, happy is that people, whose God is the LORD.

145

I will extol thee, my God, O king; and I will bless thy name for ever and ever. 145:2 Every day will I bless thee; and I will praise thy name for ever and ever. 145:3 Great is the LORD, and greatly to be praised; and his greatness is unsearchable. 145:4 One generation shall praise thy works to another, and shall declare thy mighty acts. 145:5 I will speak of the glorious honour of thy majesty, and of thy wondrous works. 145:6 And men shall speak of the might of thy terrible acts: and I will declare thy greatness. 145:7 They shall abundantly utter the memory of thy great goodness, and shall sing of thy righteousness. 145:8 The **LORD** is gracious, and full of compassion; slow to anger, and of great mercy. 145:9 The **LORD** is good to all: and his tender mercies are over all his works. 145:10 All thy works shall praise thee, **O LORD**; and thy saints shall bless thee. 145:11 They shall speak of the glory of thy kingdom, and talk of thy power; 145:12 To make known to the sons of men his mighty acts, and the glorious majesty of his kingdom. 145:13 Thy kingdom is an everlasting kingdom, and thy dominion endureth throughout all generations. 145:14 The **LORD** upholdeth all that fall, and raiseth up all those that be bowed down. 145:15 The eyes of all wait upon thee; and thou givest them their meat in due season. 145:16 Thou openest thine hand, and satisfiest the desire of every living thing. 145:17 The **LORD** is righteous in all his ways, and holy in all his works. 145:18 The **LORD** is nigh unto all them that call upon him, to all that call upon him in truth. 145:19 He will fulfil the desire of them that fear him: he also will hear their cry, and will save them. 145:20 The **LORD** preserveth all them that love him: but all the wicked will he destroy. 145:21 My mouth shall speak the praise of the **LORD**: and let all flesh bless his holy name for ever and ever.

Praise ye the LORD. Praise the LORD, O my soul. 146:2 While I live will I praise the LORD: I will sing praises unto my God while I have any being. 146:3 Put not your trust in princes, nor in the son of man, in whom there is no help. 146:4 His breath goeth forth, he returneth to his earth; in that very day his thoughts perish. 146:5 Happy is he that hath the God of Jacob for his help, whose hope is in the LORD his God: 146:6 Which made heaven, and earth, the sea, and all that therein is: which keepeth truth for ever: 146:7 Which executeth judgment for the oppressed: which giveth food to the hungry. The LORD looseth the prisoners: 146:8 The LORD openeth the eyes of the blind: the LORD raiseth them that are bowed down: the LORD loveth the righteous: 146:9 The LORD preserveth the strangers; he relieveth the fatherless and widow: but the way of the wicked he turneth upside down. 146:10 The LORD shall reign for ever, even thy God, O Zion, unto all generations. Praise ye the LORD.

Praise ye the **LORD**: for it is good to sing praises unto our God; for it is pleasant; and praise is comely. 147:2 The **LORD** doth build up Jerusalem: he gathereth together the outcasts of Israel. 147:3 He healeth the broken in heart, and bindeth up their wounds. 147:4 He telleth the number of the stars; he calleth them all by their names. 147:5 Great is our Lord, and of great power: his understanding is infinite. 147:6 The **LORD** lifteth up the meek: he casteth the wicked down to the ground. 147:7 Sing unto the **LORD** with thanksgiving; sing praise upon the harp unto our God: 147:8 Who covereth the heaven with clouds, who prepareth rain for the earth, who maketh grass to grow upon the mountains. 147:9 He giveth to the beast his food, and to the young ravens which cry. 147:10 He delighteth not in the strength of the horse: he taketh not pleasure in the legs of a man. 147:11 The **LORD** taketh pleasure in them that fear him, in those that hope in his mercy. 147:12 Praise the **LORD**, O Jerusalem; praise thy God, O Zion. 147:13 For he hath strengthened the bars of thy gates; he hath blessed thy children within thee. 147:14 He maketh peace in thy borders, and filleth thee with the finest of the wheat. 147:15 He sendeth forth his commandment upon earth: his word runneth very swiftly. 147:16 He giveth snow like wool: he scattereth the hoarfrost like ashes. 147:17 **H**e casteth forth his ice like morsels: who can stand before his cold? 147:18 **H**e sendeth out his word, and melteth them: he causeth his wind to blow, and the waters flow. 147:19 **H**e sheweth his word unto Jacob, his statutes and his judgments unto Israel. 147:20 **H**e hath not dealt so with any nation: and as for his judgments, they have not known them. Praise ye the **LORD**.

148

Praise ye the **LORD**. Praise ye the **LORD** from the heavens: praise him in the heights. 148:2 **P**raise ye him, all his angels: praise ye him, all his hosts. 148:3 **P**raise ye him, sun and moon: praise him, all ye stars of light. 148:4 **P**raise him, ye heavens of heavens, and ye waters that be above the heavens. 148:5 **L**et them praise the name of the **LORD**: for he commanded, and they were created. 148:6 **H**e hath also stablished them for ever and ever: he hath made a decree which shall not pass. 148:7 **P**raise the **LORD** from the earth, ye dragons, and all deeps: 148:8 **F**ire, and hail; snow, and vapours; stormy wind fulfilling his word: 148:9 Mountains, and all hills; fruitful trees, and all cedars: 148:10 Beasts, and all cattle; creeping things, and flying fowl: 148:11 Kings of the earth, and all people; princes, and all judges of the earth: 148:12 Both young men, and maidens; old men, and children: 148:13 Let them praise the name of the **LORD**: for his name alone is excellent; his glory is above the earth and heaven. 148:14 He also exalteth the horn of his people, the praise of all his saints; even of the children of Israel, a people near unto him. Praise ye the **LORD**.

149

Praise ye the **LORD**. Sing unto the **LORD** a new song, and his praise in the congregation of saints. 149:2 Let Israel rejoice in him that made him: let the children of Zion be joyful in their King. 149:3 Let them praise his name in the dance: let them sing praises unto him with the timbrel and harp. 149:4 For the **LORD** taketh pleasure in his people: he will beautify the meek with salvation. 149:5 Let the saints be joyful in glory: let them sing aloud upon their beds. 149:6 Let the high praises of God be in their mouth, and a two-edged sword in their hand; 149:7 To execute vengeance upon the heathen, and punishments upon the people; 149:8 To bind their kings with chains, and their nobles with fetters of iron; 149:9 To execute upon them the judgment written: this honour have all his saints. Praise ye the **LORD**.

150

Praise ye the **LORD**. Praise God in his sanctuary: praise him in the firmament of his power. 150:2 Praise him for his mighty acts: praise him according to his excellent greatness. 150:3 Praise him with the sound of the trumpet: praise him with the psaltery and harp. 150:4 Praise him with the timbrel and dance: praise him with stringed instruments and organs. 150:5 Praise him upon the loud cymbals: praise him upon the high sounding cymbals. 150:6 Let every thing that hath breath praise the **LORD**. Praise ye the **LORD**.